A Feminist Reading of Debt

Mapping Social Reproduction Theory

Series editors Tithi Bhattacharya, Professor of South Asian History and the Director of Global Studies at Purdue University; and Susan Ferguson, Associate Professor, Faculty of Liberal Arts, Wilfrid Laurier University

Capitalism is a system of exploitation and oppression. This series uses the insights of social reproduction theory to deepen our understanding of the intimacy of that relationship, and the contradictions within it, past and present. The books include empirical investigations of the ways in which social oppressions of race, sexuality, ability, gender and more inhabit, shape and are shaped by the processes of creating labour power for capital. The books engage a critical exploration of social reproduction, enjoining debates about the theoretical and political tools required to challenge capitalism today.

Also available

Social Reproduction Theory:
Remapping Class, Recentering Oppression
Edited by Tithi Bhattacharya

Women and Work:
Feminism, Labour, and Social Reproduction
Susan Ferguson

Disasters and Social Reproduction:
Crisis Response between the State and Community
Peer Illner

Social Reproduction Theory and the Socialist Horizon:
Work, Power and Political Strategy
Aaron Jaffe

A Feminist Reading of Debt

Lucí Cavallero and Verónica Gago

Translated by Liz Mason-Deese

Foreword by Tithi Bhattacharya

First published 2021 by Pluto Press
345 Archway Road, London N6 5AA

www.plutobooks.com

This book has been selected to receive financial assistance from English PEN's 'PEN Translates!' programme, supported by Arts Council England. English PEN exists to promote literature and our understanding of it, to uphold writers' freedoms around the world, to campaign against the persecution and imprisonment of writers for stating their views, and to promote the friendly co-operation of writers and the free exchange of ideas. www.englishpen.org

Work published within the framework of "Sur" Translation Support Program of the Ministry of Foreign Affairs and Worship of the Argentine Republic. Obra editada en el marco del Programa "Sur" de Apoyo a las Traducciones del Ministerio de Relaciones Exteriores y Culto de la República Argentina.

British Library Cataloguing in Publication Data
A catalogue record for this book is available from the British Library

ISBN   978 0 7453 4171 2   Hardback
ISBN   978 0 7453 4172 9   Paperback
ISBN   978 1 7868 0846 2   PDF eBook
ISBN   978 1 7868 0848 6   Kindle eBook
ISBN   978 1 7868 0847 9   EPUB eBook

Typeset by Stanford DTP Services, Northampton, England

Simultaneously printed in the United Kingdom and United States of America

Contents

Foreword

Tithi Bhattacharya

I grew up in the foothills of the Himalayas, in a region called the Terai, where wild mountain rivers and low clouds watered in equal measure dense, Sal forests. As a child I remember the smell of the thick Sal leaves, my feet remember their soft crunch on forest floors, the slanted late afternoon light playing tricks on you and revealing flitting animals behind thick trees. But the politician who came to our small town one summer told us that our forests were "valuable," the trees could, when cut down and sold, repay India's IMF loan. Our wild forests—our Sal trees, our cheetahs, elephants, and monkeys—were suddenly yoked to a register of alien comprehension. The forest was no longer a concrete provider for local communities and a habitat for multiple living beings, it was suddenly connected to a world market through abstract relations of indebtedness, power and violence.

I am grateful to Lucí Cavallero and Verónica Gago for making sense of that moment that so many of us in the global south in the first wave of the SAP (Structural Adjustment Programs) found so incomprehensible.

This book is thus primarily about making sense. Under capitalism, abstract mechanisms of the market have concrete consequences in the lives of the dispossessed. But those mechanisms, whether they are the intangible extraction of surplus labor on the shopfloor or the opaque financial operations of a subprime mortgage, remain obscured from the vision of those whom they affect and harm. Cavallero and Gago follow in the best traditions of left scholarship in making legible those operations precisely so that they can be resisted.

Under their clear analytic stewardship, we begin to understand the real purpose of capitalist debt, not simply as an operation that creates profit on the backs of the indebted but that produces obedience through financial terror. The book traces how debt organizes our lifeworld whereby we are forced to go into debt to have a home, to pay for healthcare or get an education. Simply put, debt tethers our lifemaking needs to the logic of accumulation. A 2018 report[1] by the UN Independent Expert

---

1. www.brettonwoodsproject.org/2018/12/bretton-woods-institutions-instrumental-gender-approach-ignores-structural-elephant-in-the-room/

on Foreign Debt and Human Rights notes how decades of debt-induced austerity cuts to social services mean that women in poor households now spend significantly more of their time performing unpaid care work than women in non-poor households. Precisely, then, because it is social reproduction processes that are most disfigured by debt, we need a feminist reading of debt.

Cavallero and Gago do not simply make the superficial observation that women, due to their relationship to social reproduction tasks, are most harmed by debt operations. Instead, *A Feminist Reading of Debt* offers a feminist diagnostic of capitalist finance itself. The first theoretical movement for such an investigation is visibilizing debt and its violence. As the authors show, taking "debt out of the closet ... means showing the differential way in which debt operates for women, for lesbians, and for trans people." Such an inquiry demands that we be attentive to the "*differential of exploitation*" that is created among the indebted, "those of us who spend all day managing accounts are women, housewives, female heads of households, formal workers, popular economy workers, sex workers, migrants, inhabitants of the villas or favelas, Black and Indigenous women, travestis, campesinas, or students." Most importantly, such a methodology of "visibilizing debt and showing its sexual and gender difference" are ways of "*removing its power of abstraction*".

Throughout the text, the authors perform many such acts of disclosure. In one of the most powerful sections of the book an activist with the unemployed workers' organization, Federación de Organizaciones de Base, relates how loan companies situate themselves strategically at the nodal points of everyday lifemaking, "In the neighborhood ... the school exit ... the clinic where you take your children to the doctor or to the market where people are constantly circulating." For the loan companies all that is required for eligibility is proof of state assistance for welfare. If someone qualifies for state benefits, they qualify for a loan. In other words, the public benefits of the capitalist state are used as a pivot for indebtedness to private companies. In what the authors call financial terrorism, this financialization of everyday life "forces the poorest sectors (and now not only those sectors) go into debt to pay for food and medication and to finance the payment of basic services in installments with incredibly high interest rates."

The book, its robust defense of disorder, and even the form in which it presents itself, invites discussion and debate. So, when I say I have some disagreements with Cavallero and Gago's conceptualization of financialization and its role in capitalist ordering, I say so in the same spirit that animates feminist assemblies: disagreement in the secure knowledge that we will find each other on the same side of the barricades.

One of my disagreements is rooted in the authors' framing of dispossession. Cavallero and Gago hold firm to David Harvey's framework of accumulation by dispossession which then informs their analysis of the deeply colonial nature of debt and dispossession. I belong to the school of thought that ascribes perhaps a more sinister history to accumulation. One that believes that in the neoliberal era, capital accumulation has combined processes of dispossession with expanded reproduction in a way that, while still reliant on nation states, nevertheless embedded capital in transnational networks of production as never before. In other words, I believe dispossession and expanded reproduction to be of closer kin than the "accumulation by dispossession" framework allows, which brings me to my second disagreement. If we theorize dispossession to be dominant over expanded reproduction then there is a danger of underestimating the potential of solidarity between struggles at the point of production and those that erupt away from such points. Uprisings such as the Nigerian general strike of 2012 and the Indian Farmers' protests of 2020–21 come to mind, as social eruptions that began as social reproduction protests in communities and neighborhoods, the protests against gasoline subsidy in Nigeria and anti-farmer laws in India, but then blossomed into classwide rebellion and brought workplaces to a standstill.

To emphasize the unity of these twin processes of capitalist accumulation is to also draw attention to the possibilities of international solidarity. The very global networks of debt and dispossession that bind communities are the same ones that bind workplaces with the iron law of capitalist compulsion. Sometimes the culprits are even the same companies! BlackRock, the largest holder of Argentinian debt, is also the power behind Emmanuel Macron's pension reforms, and the company that is forcing the Mexican government to increase the retirement age for workers.

It is in the tracing of this filigreed web of international solidarity that this book is at its most powerful. As activists in the massive feminist uprisings in Argentina since 2016, the authors analyze struggle from the perspective of these mobilizations and therefore arrive at truths about the social form that perhaps a solely academic view would fall short of. This specifically feminist perspective on debt allows the authors to powerfully weave together issues of sexist violence and economic violence in the

x · A FEMINIST READING OF DEBT

same interpretive frame. To explain, for example, how mortgage debt immobilizes women and forces them to remain in situations of domestic violence while financialization of everyday life disciplines women and LGBTQ people to accept capital's "decision-making power over ... bodies and territories." But what makes this analysis rooted in feminist activism, not just in theory, is the authors' insistence that there is a connection between these issues, thereby "initiating subterranean links and intersections that became part of a new common vocabulary and an unprecedented form of collective comprehension." Instead of being disciplined by debt, the authors reiterate the feminist slogan "the debt is owed to us", thereby making this book, in the last instance, one that calls for and opens up an insubordinate future.

Translator's Note

It would be difficult to overestimate the effect of debt on the everyday lives of women, lesbians, and trans people in Argentina. Living in Argentina as I translated this book, I witnessed firsthand the invasion of debt into every part of life. Buying food is marked by constant, yet unpredictable inflation: never knowing how much a liter of milk will cost, only that it will be more than the day before, juggling multiple credit cards to be able to get the best deals and most affordable payment plans. Remember on Tuesdays if you use your Banco Ciudad credit card, you get a discount at Día grocery stores, but on Wednesdays you have to use your Tarjeta Galicia ... and so on. Staying on top of the deals and discounts, managing a series of cards and accounts, making decisions based on guessing inflation and rate increases ... all of this extra work (and associated anxiety!) falls primarily on women and profoundly shapes everyday life and your plans for the future. You become forced to take on any job, under any conditions to pay off debts, debt ties you to abusive living situations, limits your access to medical treatments or to education. Reproduction becomes impossible without debt.

But something else stands out as well: the everyday collective responses to debt. For example, I participated in a rotating credit circle with comrades from my political collective and put a friend's debt on my debit card to save them from the gas company's exorbitant interest rates. I participated in protests against usurious lending agencies and financial institutions. These ways of collectively tackling debt often emerge directly from feminist organizing practices and are part of a process of politicizing debt that has been sparked by the feminist movement.

Over the last five years Argentina's feminist movement has exhibited an unprecedented vibrancy and vitality. This vitality is seen in its mass mobilizations: one million people surrounding congress to demand the legalization of abortion or hundreds of thousands marching to demand justice for femicides. It is seen in the series of feminist strikes that have taken place since October 2016, women, lesbians, and trans and non-binary people withdrawing *all* their labor from a system that completely disregards our lives. That vibrancy is also seen in the everyday practices of feminists organizing mutual aid networks, self-defense groups, and grassroots communications platforms, feminists organizing and transforming every moment and space of daily life. And it is seen in the intellectual vibrancy of feminisms – it has given rise to unprecedented intellectual production that stems from the encounters between heterogeneous subject positions and experiences, from a feminist methodology that starts from particular experiences to trace and analyze their connection. This methodology has enabled new ways of understanding the relation between economic violence, state violence, and gender-based violence.

Thus, this gives us the first key to reading this book: as the outcome of a collective reflection, of a knowledge produced in movement, from feminist encounters and assemblies, from Lucí and Vero's own involvement in a range of activities from the Ni Una Menos Collective and organizing the feminist strikes, to struggles around affordable housing and against pension reform. The issue of debt arises not as an abstract condition to define a form of governmentality, but from the lived experiences of women, lesbians, travestis, trans and non-binary people who put those experiences in common as part of a feminist methodology. Thus this book can be read as a map of these specific experiences of indebtedness and from there a map of connections emerges. The practice of the assembly plays a key role in this methodology, bringing together different subject positions and experiences, and questions, challenges, and transforms all of them in the process of collective knowledge production. It was in these assemblies that the issue of debt emerged as a line that connects the experiences of different women and feminized bodies, as a common problem, albeit in different forms.

This debt is inserted into all areas of everyday life. And as Lucí and Vero show here, recently new forms of debt have started directly targeting the most vulnerable of society, sectors that previously were not considered worthy of financial exploitation. Similar to subprime mortgages in the United States, in Argentina banks and informal credit agencies offer loans to those without credit history, charging higher and variable interest rates to make up for the bank's supposed extra risk. Often this credit is even offered to people without any formal income. How is this possible? Because of a revalorization of the popular economy, of all the forms of labor and value production that exceed the formal waged economy, that include all the multiple ways of getting by that people invent to survive in times of crisis. This is the second key for reading this book, as a map of contemporary forms of labor and value production, in which reproductive labor and other forms of feminized labor play a central role.

Here Argentina's particular situation becomes crucial. In the midst of the country's economic crisis in 2001, the unemployed workers' movements forced the state to directly provide them with money, an income, bypassing the labor market and deciding for themselves what would be considered valuable work. At the same time, people experimented with myriad ways of getting by, with cooperatives, self-managed enterprises, collective forms of social reproduction in community kitchens, healthcare centers, and schools. It is this heterogeneous popular economy, including the economy of state subsidies, that finance now seeks to exploit. This book, by mapping out those forms of labor, is able to specifically show how debt *extracts* value from social reproduction and from feminized labor and also reinforces and produces gendered differentials. A feminist reading of debt highlights social reproduction as a terrain of struggle, a struggle over valorization and extraction and over how reproduction is organized and to what effect.

But this feminist reading of debt also goes beyond anthropological and sociological accounts of how debt affects women, beyond the well-known arguments of how structural adjustment privatizes state services and leads to more work for women. Rather than seeing women and feminized bodies as solely victims, trapped in cycles of debt, without autonomy or agency to resist, a feminist reading of debt emphasizes already existing struggles against debt and explores how we might expand that disobedience. This perspective of resistance is the third key for reading this book.

How can a feminist reading of debt help us understand and fight against these multiple forms of debt that have become so ingrained in our everyday lives? First, by taking debt out of the closet, by mapping it and discussing, challenging the feelings of shame and personal guilt associated with debt that hinder its politicization. Politicizing debt also means tracing the connections between different types of debts, between national debts and household debts, between debt in one sphere and another. By doing so, this book constructs a countermap of all the places where debt can be resisted and the alliances that can be formed in that resistance. Thus, it serves as a practical guide to disobedience.

This disobedience takes on a multiplicity of forms, from collectively organizing ways to meet people's needs without going into debt to alternative forms of credit such as rotating credit circles, to protesting against usurious credit agencies and utility companies. The interviews that conclude the book introduce us to some of those forms of disobedience, from some of the groups most affected by debt, including incarcerated women, campesinas, and the young and precariously employed. What these interviews show is how disobeying debt, and the mandates it seeks to impose, is primarily a matter of collective organization, even in situations of extreme precarity or vulnerability. And thus, we imagine that their stories will resonate with those affected by debt in other parts of the globe, from student debt to medical debt and consumer debt, to the debts imposed by international financial institutions and foreign governments.

Of course these struggles against debt are not limited to Argentina. Some of the most powerful uprisings of the last year, in Chile and Ecuador, directly took on the issue of debt – both with the International Monetary Fund (IMF) and how that debt spills over into women's lives, showing how this analysis and agenda is already transnational. Recent uprisings in Puerto Rico have also focused on opposing the colonial debt imposed on the island. In the United States, of course, the situation of household debt is not unfamiliar, whether from student loans, healthcare debt, mortgage payments, or consumer debt, debt structures and limits everyday life and one's projections of the future. Occupy Wall Street and many of its offshoots, the student movement, and anti-eviction movements have all struggled against debt in different ways. What this book hopefully offers to these movements is a methodology for connecting experiences and struggles and for bringing a feminist lens to understanding how debt exploits reproduction and produces gendered differentials.

We hope that these stories can provide inspiration, as well as concrete clues for organizing, for all those affected by debt. And that the feminist methodology presented here, of mapping debt based on concrete struggles, recognizing the multiplicity of labor and forms of extraction and the centrality of social reproduction, can serve as a tool in other contexts and situations. The first edition of this work, published in Argentina in 2019, was presented, discussed, and debated in a variety of spaces from union halls to community centers, to student groups and to groups of housewives, to campesina organizations and bank workers. These presentations served to expand the struggle against debt, spreading it to more sectors and areas, and also to deepen the analysis, which is presented here in this extended version. We hope that this translation will give rise to more conversations about how each one of us is affected by debt and what the fight against debt's mandate looks like in each specific place. In that sense, this translation aims to be another step in the process of connecting different struggles against debt in a feminist register.

Liz Mason-Deese

Preface

This book condenses the encounter between a process of politicizing debt carried out by the feminist movement and a series of investigations based out of the public university and other spaces of militant debate and research. It was first published in Argentina in February 2019 and over the course of that year it turned into a medium for a multiplicity of political interventions and conversations. Through these interventions and conversations it continued to grow, ultimately doubling its pages to compose this new version.

We have presented the book and used it as a tool for debate and education in unions, universities, craft markets, peasant organizations, and feminist assemblies. But it also rapidly fueled transnational exchanges: we have discussed it with comrades in Chile, Mexico, the United States, Brazil (where it has already been translated by Helena Vargas and published by Criação Humana), Germany, Puerto Rico, Italy (translated by Nicolás Martino and published by Ombre Corte), Belgium, and Ecuador.

Simultaneously, the feminist perspective on debt was interwoven with other issues, spreading and deepening as a common language across a diverse array of struggles ranging from resistance to urban development of the slums in Buenos Aires to the repudiation of the pension reform. In 2017, we – as part of the Ni Una Menos Collective – launched the slogan "We want ourselves alive, free, and debt free" (a few months after the first international feminist strike). This way of bringing together the issue of sexist violence and economic violence has become a powerful interpretative key for the social movement. Unions gradually appropriated the slogan, as did workers who had been laid off as well as students. This has given rise to a diagnosis of what we call "financial violence" based on each unique struggle and in the heat of the feminist strikes, but, even more so, it has opened a horizon of investigation about what disobedience to financial invasion means in daily life.

Therefore, we want to emphasize that this dynamic has changed how austerity plans – which the IMF has once again imposed through the modality of foreign debt – are interpreted and confronted. With the feminist revolution, the anticolonial tradition on our continent has been given a new life. Thus, it does not seem coincidental that in the 2020 International Feminist Strike in Argentina, we went on strike and mobilized under a common motto that synthesizes this journey through which the feminist movement has confronted the government of finance. The slogan says "the debt is owed to us," inverting the terms of who are the creditors and who are the debtors, and opening up a horizon of insubordination and antagonism between debt and finance. Here and there it is feminism in its everyday revolution that has updated and illuminated the modes in which capital today needs a specific form of violence against certain bodies and territories to effect its valorization. And it has done so on the streets, in homes, and in plazas, reinventing a revolutionary spatiality.

Dialogue with Silvia Federici has been fundamental for our elaborations. Her perspective on social reproduction and financialization is the foundation of much of our reasoning. Additionally, we have been nourished by personal political exchanges with her during the feminist tide in Argentina.

In relation to the first edition in Spanish, published by the Rosa Luxemburg Foundation, here we have made a substantial expansion, bringing together concrete interventions that continue broadening the debate on debt (debt and abortion, debt and food crisis, debt and care, etc.), as well as the way in which the conjuncture of Argentina's change in government was marked by these debates. In the same way, it was also notable how the issue of debt was directly connected to uprisings on our continent in 2019 (particularly in Chile and Puerto Rico, but also in Colombia and Ecuador). Therefore, we want this edition to be a living book, capable of including everything generated by the original book, but also able to take advantage of this new version to inscribe it within the political work that the feminist movement is carrying out in multiple geographies and scales and that has shown a phenomenal intensity over the last year. We hope that this translation into English can also be a tool of struggle for the desires of disobedience in a transborder tide.

We are grateful that this book is being published in the Mapping Social Reproduction Theory Series, coordinated by Tithi Bhattacharya and Susan Ferguson. It is more of an inclusion-intrusion, since many of the hypotheses developed here challenge some of the proposals of Social Reproduction Theory. We consider it a way of deepening the debate within a shared political commitment. We want to thank Liz Mason-

Deese for her rigorous translation and also the encounter with David Shulman and Camille Barbagallo that made this edition possible.

And last, but not least: we write this prologue in the midst of the pandemic, which has brought up the debate and urgency of a feminist reading of debt in new circumstances. We hope that this book can also be a tool in the midst of this civilizational crisis in which we are enmeshed.

Buenos Aires, September 2020

Introduction:
Taking Debt Out of the Closet

This book systematizes our personal and collective investigations carried out over the past few years within the public and free university in Argentina, as well as in spaces of militant research, particularly as members of the Ni Una Menos Collective. Our investigations and activism show that there is an urgent need to develop a specifically feminist analysis of finance. Here we do so by bringing together methodological elements, political hypotheses, and narratives of practices elaborated by the feminist movement that are challenging finance.

This material is inscribed within the horizon of the organizational process of the international feminist strikes that, since 2016, have allowed us to develop these conversations through situating ourselves in concrete actions. Like the process of the contemporary feminist movement itself, this elaboration is *open*, ongoing. Here we provide a perspective on feminist economics through synthesizing idea-forces that function as original and stimulating coordinates that can be useful for further collective research. This feminist reading of debt is only possible because we have been able to discuss finance in terms of conflict and, therefore, in terms of the self-defense of our autonomy. That is what allows us to shout "We want ourselves alive, free, and debt free!"

As fascism is imposed at a regional and global level, it constructs the feminist movement as its internal enemy and produces a new type of alliance between capital and fascist micropolitics. Thus, it becomes imperative to understand how debt functions as the privileged apparatus of new forms of exploitation and how it is articulated with sexist violence.

In the 1980s, debt disciplined the democratic transitions from dictatorships in Latin America, as countries were forced to orient their economies toward repaying the debt taken out during authoritarian regimes. In the 1990s, the "Washington Consensus" of neoliberal reforms pushed new thresholds of debt, and today we are facing a forceful relaunching of financial colonization of our region, combined with increasingly intensive situations of poverty and dispossession of resources.

We hope this material can be used in multiple ways, in debates with all types of political, union, community, educational, and feminist organizations. Our desire is that it serves as an excuse for initiating new exchanges and deepening a feminist diagnostic of the crisis of the present.

DIAGNOSING FORMS OF VIOLENCE

In recent years the feminist movement has not only been characterized by its massiveness in terms of the number of people on the streets, but also for its capacity to open up new debates and to circulate concepts and diagnoses about various issues. These issues range from abortion to debt, in a broad, heterogeneous, and complex arch. But there is another step: it *connected* those problematics, initiating subterranean links and intersections that became part of a new common vocabulary and an unprecedented form of collective comprehension. Thus, it is more than an agenda or set of demands (which it also is). It implies the politicization of issues that were long considered to be marginal or only of interest to a minority, or the exclusive realm of experts. It also involves connecting zones of the exploitation of life that appear to be disconnected or are treated as independent variables by mainstream economics.

Let's start with the general diagnostic. The feminist movement has demonstrated how the precarity caused by neoliberal policies constitutes a specific economy of violence in which femicide and travesticides are its culminating scene. And it has put that economy of violence on the public agenda. We could synthesize it as such: we have developed a multilayered comprehension of the different forms of violence that also complicates and enriches the challenges for dismantling it.

We were able to conclude that femicides and travesticides are political crimes because the connection had previously been drawn between gender-based violence and labor violence, between racist violence and institutional violence, between the violence of the legal system and economic and financial violence. What explodes as "domestic violence" cannot be understood without this map of the whole, without this diagram of links. When we speak of violence against women, lesbians, and trans people we are getting at the heart of the system of capitalist violence, the violence necessary to sustain it in its current phase of cruelty.

It is this method of connection that is properly feminist, which makes intersectionality into a concrete politics: understanding how debt organizes obedience at the level of the state also means rendering visible how it organizes daily life in each household. It implies disputing decision-making power over our bodies and territories in a demand that simultaneously calls for the right to abortion and repudiates extractivism. It manages to show how the heterosexual norm is articulated as one of the criteria in how the state assigns subsidized housing, going hand in hand with real estate speculation in urban development projects of popular neighborhoods and slums, and so forth.

EXPLOITATION AND DIFFERENCE

What does it mean to take debt out of the closet? To take each individual's, each household's, each family's debt out of the closet, first we have to talk about it. It means narrating it and conceptualizing it in order to understand how it functions; investigating how it is interwoven with different economies. It means making visible how it extracts value from certain forms of life and how it intervenes in processes of production and reproduction of life. It means asking: In which territories does it gain strength? What types of obedience does it produce? Taking it out of the closet means *making it visible and situating it as a common problem*, de-individualizing it. Because taking debt out of the closet involves challenging its power to shame and guilt and its power to function as a "private issue," which we can only face by managing our accounts alone.

Taking debt out of the closet also means showing the differential way in which debt operates for women, for lesbians, and for trans people. It requires inquiring into *the differential of exploitation* that is created when the indebted – those of us who spend all day managing accounts – are women, housewives, female heads of households, formal workers, popular economy workers, sex workers, migrants, inhabitants of the *villas* or *favelas* (informal settlements or slums), Black and Indigenous women, travestis, campesinas, or students. Both moves – visibilizing debt and showing its sexual and gender difference – are ways of *removing its power of abstraction*. Both moves are also inscribed within a geopolitics: the subjectivity of an indebted North American private university student is not the same as that of a subsidized worker in a cooperative in the largely migrant neighborhood of Flores in Buenos Aires.

Therefore, it is not merely a matter of confirming "the making of the indebted man," as Maurizio Lazzarato (2012) does, postulating a universal subjectivity of the debtor-creditor relation, but rather of highlighting two fundamental elements that he does not take into account:

gender differences and the power of disobedience. On the one hand, gender difference operates differently in regards to debt. That is due to several reasons, since that difference supposes: (1) a particular form of moralization directed toward women and feminized bodies; (2) a differential of exploitation due to the corresponding relations of sub-ordination; (3) a specific relation between debt and reproductive tasks; (4) the concrete impact of sexist violence, to which debt is connected; and (5) fundamental variations in possibilities "for the future" involving financial obligation in the case of feminized bodies. On the other hand, we want to highlight the possibility of disobeying debt and, in particular, the practical forms of defiance that are being pushed by the feminist movement (we will come back to this issue in the section "How to Disobey Finance").

This does not deny the fact that debt is a transversal apparatus of exploitation (Lazzarato 2015), which operates by capturing the production of the common (Terranova 2017). However, we see a critical need to affirm that *there is not a singular subjectivity of indebtedness that can be universalized nor a sole debtor-creditor relation that can be separated from concrete situations and especially from sexual, gender, racial, and locational difference, precisely because debt does not homogenize those differences, but rather exploits them.* The way in which debt *lands* in diverse territories, economies, and conflicts is central, not a secondary feature.

In this sense, *taking debt out of the closet is a feminist response to debt:* it is to de-enclose it, de-privatize it, and give it a body, a voice, and a territory. Then, building on that, it investigates experiments in modes of disobedience. Therefore, there is a third move (after its deconfinement and corporealization) that is inseparable from this feminist gesture: *conspiring to defy debt.* This is not only an analytical perspective, but rather an analysis that itself forms part of this program of disobedience. Taking debt out of the closet is a political move against guilt, against the abstraction exercised by the domination of finance, and against the moral argument that women are "good payers," which is used to legitimize targeting feminized bodies as the favored responsible subjects of financial obligation.

A Feminist Reading of Debt

When we speak of debt, we place particular emphasis on private debt or what we will call indebted household economies (a term that we will problematize and broaden). Today, finance lands in household economies, in popular economies, and waged economies through mass indebtedness and it does so in ways that are specific to each one of those economies.

Our perspective is based on a tripartite wager. First, we want to highlight the fact that we cannot understand debt in its contemporary form only by looking at public debt (debt taken out by the state), while ignoring indebtedness in everyday life. Second, it is politically necessary for social movements and organizations to take the issue of debt into account in their resistance practices. And third, talking about debt in everyday life brings us to a strategic task: tracing the links between debt and sexist violence. By doing this, contemporary feminist struggles are leading a movement of the *politicization and collectivization* of the issue of finance (Cavallero and Gago 2018).

But, what is a *feminist reading* of debt? Here we start with a brief practical guide.

1. A feminist reading of debt proposes concrete bodies and narratives of its operation in opposition to financial abstraction.

Finance boasts of being abstract, of belonging to the sky of mysterious quotes, of functioning according to logics that cannot be comprehended by common people. It tries to present itself as a true black box, in which decisions are made in a mathematical, algorithmic way about what has value and what does not. By narrating how it functions in households, popular (largely non-waged), and waged economies, we defy its power of abstraction, its attempt to be unfathomable. That becomes clear in the interviews included in this book. Debt is a concrete mechanism that forces small agricultural producers to become dependent on agro-toxins. Debt is an expression of the rising costs and financialization of basic services. Debt is an apparatus that connects the inside and outside of prison, while prison itself is shown to be a system of debt. Debt is what you incur when abortion is criminalized. Debt is what drives popular consumption when exorbitant interest rates cause domestic life, health, and community bonds to explode. Debt is what enables illegal economies to recruit workers at any price. Debt incurred by young people, even "before" entering the labor market or in hyper-precarious jobs (since they are given a credit card along with their state benefits and first paycheck) appears as an apparatus of capture and precaritization of those very incomes. Debt is what provides basic infrastructure for life: health services that are inaccessible, supplies for when a child is born, purchasing a motorcycle to be able to work in food delivery. Debt is a way of guaranteeing access to housing. Debt is the resource that appears when one is faced with emergencies and confronted by the loss of other support networks. Debt is a mechanism of generalized dispossession of migrant and Black populations. Debt is what ties together dependence on violent family relations.

2. A feminist reading of debt involves detecting how debt is linked to violence against feminized bodies.

Drawing on concrete narratives of indebtedness, the link between debt and sexist violence becomes clear. Debt is what does not allow us to say no when we want to say no. Debt is what ties us to a *future* of violent relations from which we want to flee. Debt forces us to maintain broken relationships, which we continue to be locked into because of medium or long-term financial obligations. Debt is what impedes economic autonomy, even in feminized economies in which women play leading roles. At the same time, we cannot ignore its *ambivalence*: debt also enables certain movements. In other words, debt not only *fixes in place*; in some cases, it enables movement. We can think, for example, about those who go into debt in order to migrate. Or those who take out debt to start their own economic project. Or who take out debt to flee. But one thing is clear: whether as *fixation* or as the possibility of *movement*, debt exploits an availability to future work; it forces you to accept any type of work due to the pre-existing obligation of debt. Debt compulsively makes one have to accept more flexible labor conditions and, in that sense, it is an efficient apparatus of exploitation. Debt then organizes an economy of obedience that is nothing more or less than a specific economy of violence.

3. A feminist reading of debt maps and analyzes forms of work in a feminist register, rendering visible domestic, reproductive, and community labor as spaces of valorization that finance sets out to exploit.

The international strikes of women, lesbians, trans people, and travestis allowed for debating and making visible a map of the heterogeneity of labor from a feminist perspective. Based on diverse feminisms, *a method of struggle emerged that corresponds to the current composition of what we call work*, including migrant, precarious, neighborhood, domestic, community labor. That movement also produced elements for understanding waged labor in a new way and transformed how unions themselves organize.

Adding the financial dimension allows us to now map flows of debt and complete the map of exploitation in its most dynamic, versatile, and apparently "invisible" forms. Understanding how debt extracts value from household economies and non-waged economies, those economies historically considered not to be productive, shows how financial apparatuses operate as *true mechanisms of the colonization of the reproduction of life*. It also demonstrates how debt enters into waged economies and subordinates them. Additionally, it allows us to understand how debt functions as a privileged apparatus for laundering illicit monetary flows, and, therefore, as the crucial link between illegal and legal economies.

DEBT AND SOCIAL REPRODUCTION

In Argentina, the way in which state benefits (which recognize popular economies as a source of self-managed employment) have been articulated with compulsory and individualizing bankarization over the last decade and a half has been the key condition for *financial exploitation* of "assisted" populations (Gago 2017; Gago and Roig 2019). In Argentina, the massification of social benefit packages in the early 2000s was carried out as a governmental attempt to "respond" to the crisis, at the same time as their conquest was determined by the force of social movements that were able to negotiate the corresponding work requirement. This does not mean that the wage ceases to exist, but rather that an ever greater number of people must seek prosperity without assuming the wage as their principal income. It is this reality, which emerged with the crisis, that is "stabilized" with popular economies, systematizing the new passage to proletarian micro-economies (Gago 2017). These economies are composed of *cartoneros* (informal trash pickers) and sewing workers,

market vendors and care workers, cooks and community health prac-
titioners, cleaners and small agrarian producers. Their material fabric
opens horizons where the popular and the communitarian emerge
as political dynamics that exceed the state but do not underestimate
its power.

State assistance – a wide range of welfare benefits from the Universal
Child Allowance to unemployment benefits or housing subsidies – are
usually distributed through debit cards, opening the door to other forms
of bankarization. This occurs in a context in which the wage ceases to
be the privileged guarantee for indebtedness, to be replaced by these
state benefits, which start to function as the state guarantee for taking
out credit for populations that are largely unwaged. In other words,
showing proof of benefits is enough to be offered a loan by different
financial entities. Thus, financial mediation takes mass indebtedness as
its preferred apparatus, which is driven by the same social subsidies that
the state hands over to the so-called "vulnerable sectors" (Gago 2015).

The consumption of non-durable and cheap goods – the primary
use of credit – was the motor of debt in Argentina over the last decade,
promoting forms of "citizenship by consumption": a reformulation of the
institution of citizenship, in which rights are no longer linked to waged
labor, but rather to "banking inclusion" (Gago 2015, 2017). What finance
recognizes and attempts to capture is the dynamic of subjects connected
to new forms of labor, entrepreneurship, and self-management that
emerged in the popular and poor sectors in parallel to their condemnation as surplus populations. Finance lands in subaltern territories
and ignores the political categories that speak of excluded, marginal, or
surplus to categorize and "include" these populations, those who are left
out of the world of waged labor and the "formal" market. Finance recognizes and exploits a non-waged productive fabric, which is made up
of varied forms of contracting and includes informal wages and state
benefits. The state plays a key role in the construction of an architecture
of institutional obligation: imposing compulsory banking, promoted
through the propaganda of "financial inclusion," and, ultimately, functioning as the guarantee for mass indebtedness at the hands of banks and
other financial agencies established by banks to deal with the popular
sectors, although they present themselves as being outside the financial
system, and thus are subject to even less regulation.

An entire specific section of the population that is characterized by
being migrant, informal, productive, and lacking capital is targeted for

indebtedness, which, in turn, functions as the driver for expanding that sector's capacity to consume. The relation between inclusion, money, and peripheral neighborhoods promotes a rhetoric that is the opposite of that of austerity and manages to unify inclusion and exploitation under financial apparatuses. What becomes clear is that these popular, precarious, and feminized economies, which were previously visualized as insignificant and merely subsidiary, have turned into territories that are dynamic and attractive for capital, expanding the frontiers of its valorization and creating new consumers, beyond the guarantee of the wage. Debt thus becomes an apparatus that is increasingly tied to new labor forms, which are largely not waged in the traditional sense (which does not mean that the wage does not still operate in a complementary and intermittent way).

Debt functions by structuring a compulsion to accept any type of work to pay the obligation to the future. In this sense, it drives precarization from "within." Debt puts in practice the exploitation of creativity at any price: it does not matter what work you do, all that matters is repaying your debt. The precarious, informal, and even illegal dynamic of the jobs (or forms of income) is revealed to be increasingly discontinuous while debt operates as the stable continuum that exploits that multiplicity. That temporal gap is also taken advantage of: debt becomes a coercion mechanism, forcing people to accept any working conditions, due to the fact that the financial obligation ends up "commanding" labor in the present tense. Debt then drives a molecular diffusion of that obligation that, although it is to the future, conditions the here and now, imposing ever greater velocity and violence. Debt functions and spills over into territories as a compulsory mechanism for subjugation to precarization (in the conditions, times, and violence of work), morally reinforced as an economy of obedience.

It is essential to highlight the *feminized character of these popular, precarious, and often a-legal economies in a twofold sense.* In a *quantitative* sense, because women make up the majority of those in the position of "head of household," that is, as the main family support (in families that are extended, assembled, and also imploded). And in a *qualitative* sense, in relation to the type of tasks involved, which are primarily related to labors of community care, food provision, and neighborhood cleaning and security, and, in a broader sense, to producing the infrastructure of basic services for the reproduction of life.

FINANCIAL EXTRACTIVISM AND DISPOSSESSION

There is another twist: with the increasing financialization of the reproduction of life, the reproductive relation is shown, more than ever, to be the space of valorization and accumulation par excellence. This is due to the fact that in order for finance to be able to invade and colonize the sphere of social reproduction, first it must systematically dispossess the infrastructure of public services, common resources, and the economies capable of guaranteeing autonomous reproduction (from peasant economies to self-managed economies, from cooperative elements to popular-communitarian ones).

This "democratization" of our societies, when it is left in the hands of credit (and the promise of "financial inclusion") that provides access to consumption, is nothing more or less than the consecration of the dismantling of other ways of securing resources: be they waged, self-managed, public, and/or communitarian. It is the feminist movement that has rendered this dynamic visible, challenging the language of democratic access to financial institutions that is used to promote the expansion of finance.

This phenomenon is verified very eloquently by data from the Argentine Political Economy Center (CEPA) on indebtedness in poor households in 2019.[1] According to this study, 92 percent of the existing beneficiaries of the Universal Child Allowance requested (and received) loans. That process of going into debt demonstrates how inflation, which affects the prices of food, medication, gas, electricity, and water, has created a situation in which social assistance primarily functions as a guarantee in order to take out more debt instead of as an income to cover basic needs.

Therefore, when the debt relation trickles down, the effects of debt taken out by the state pour down. That is, the dispossession and privatization required by the state's indebtedness are translated into forced indebtedness of subaltern sectors. This ends up both modifying the relation between income and debt and converting bonds of mutual aid into means of exploitation and vigilance.

---

1. Centro de Economía Política Argentina. 2019. "El 90% de los niños, niñas y adolescentes no tienen cubiertas sus necesidades de alimentación por el ingreso mensual de AUH," September, 16. https://centrocepa.com.ar/informes/232-el-90-de-los-ninos-ninas-y-adolescentes-no-tiene-cubiertas-sus-necesidades-de-alimentacion-por-el-ingreso-mensual-de-auh.html (accessed December 2, 2020).

WHAT IS DEBT?

We will propose some references to trace a map of coordinates that define debt as a mechanism of exploitation that is specific to this time. Some of the perspectives that we comment on here *develop a feminist perspective for situating their analysis.*

Debt has been defined as a mechanism of subjection and servitude, which structures the debtor-credit relation as constitutive of capitalism. Friedrich Nietzsche links the "genealogy of morals" (2014 [1987]) precisely to the mechanism of the infinite, unpayable debt and its Christian translation into terms of guilt.

Silvia Federici (2012) provides key elements for a feminist analysis of debt: she emphasizes the fragmentation of the class relation that debt produces, its role when it comes to dismantling the wage as an accumulation of the struggles that have constituted it, and the financialization of services that were the state's responsibility, such as healthcare and education. She makes a crucial connection between these problems and the exploitation of common resources and women's reproductive labor.

Maurizio Lazzarato (2012) has returned to Nietzsche to argue how the dynamic of the worker has given way to the "making of the indebted man," to explain how debt imposes a "work on the self" that directly links it to a debtor "morality." We are always in debt with something and with someone. That is, we take on responsibility and guilt for achievements and failures, ultimately, for our own entrepreneurial capacity, as a way of individualizing risk and thinking about life itself as a business.

David Graeber (2011) historicizes the economy based on the institution of debt (both public and private), particularly looking at how it functions as a mechanism of subordination of countries in the Third World as a regime of global governance.

Saskia Sassen (2014) has conceptualized finance – from debt to the financial derivatives composed, for example, of mortgages – as a preferred mechanism for the "expulsions" enacted by contemporary capitalism. Contemporary finance works, she argues, by securitizing – that is, *invading* – non-financial tasks, sectors, and spaces to relocate them within financial circuits.

Wendy Brown, in *Undoing the Demos: Neoliberalism's Stealth Revolution* (2015), dedicates ample pages to debt in the North American university system to explain a more general hypothesis: the relation between debt and neoliberalism. Detailing the way in which financial capital seeks to financialize everything, she points to the importance of debt and derivatives when it comes to "transforming neoliberal rationality itself – its formulation of markets, subjects, and rational action" (p. 70).

Frédéric Lordon (2010) studies the affective mobilization that contemporary capital requires, in which the exploitation of desire and the reward for consumption activate financial formulas in partnership with the drive of marketing.

Keeanga-Yamahtta Taylor (2016) illuminates the racist dimension of foreclosures on mortgaged homes (with subprime mortgages) during the 2008 financial crisis, in which more than 240,000 African Americans lost their homes, reinforcing gentrification processes in the main cities of the United States. To do so, the criminalization and police persecution of the Black population is assembled with indebtedness through fines, traffic offenses, and arrest warrants that complete the circuit of multiple forms of violence.

Cédric Durand (2018) explains how finance appropriates the future temporality through the dispossession and parasitism of common resources, which makes finance "sovereign" thanks to austerity policies, as well as how finance takes advantage of a juridical architecture that gives it a stability that it does not itself possess.

George Caffentzis (2018) draws a connection between micro-debts and macro-debts and details the differences between the wage and debt as divergent temporal modes of exploitation.

In general, the horizon of these recent perspectives is the problematization of the 2008 financial crisis. And the question that they lay out is related to neoliberalism's capacity to redouble its policies of austerity and structural adjustment through that same crisis. That is, they ask how neoliberalism manages to *govern the crisis through public and private debt*.

There are several analyses specifically regarding the Latin American region. In Argentina, research has focused on how finance lands in popular economies and, in particular, how indebtedness has been interwoven with social subsidies in such a way as to "skip" dependence on the wage in producing "debtors" in parallel with a feminization of labor (see Gago 2017; Gago and Roig 2019).

In Bolivia, a pioneering investigation by Graciela Toro (2010) analyzes the expansion of microcredit especially designed for women, called solidarity credit, and how it has been contested by a powerful social movement of debtors. As Maria Galindo emphasizes in the prologue to Toro's book, the bank exploits women's social networks, their relationships of friendship and family, to convert them into guarantees for debt.

Nina Madsen (2013), questioning the discourse of the formation of a "new middle class" during the progressive governments in Brazil, affirms that access to greater levels of consumption for a significant part of the population was sustained by the massive indebtedness of households and the over-exploitation of women's unremunerated labor.

César Giraldo (2017) analyzes the dismantling of social policies in Colombia and new financial forms, particularly loans, for popular economy workers.

Magdalena Villareal's (2004) investigations in Mexico are also a reference for thinking about how everyday finance organizes the social reproduction of popular classes and, in particular, the role of women in those economic forms and networks.

The case of Chile is perhaps the most pressing in the region (Ossandón 2012). According to data from 2018, households have over 70 percent of their income in debt, a record high, due to the decline in income paralleled with greater banking indebtedness.

NEW ERA: FINANCIAL TERROR

When we speak of *financial terror* we are not only referring to how banks do business with the exchange rate difference or the speculation carried out by investment funds facilitated by the government or the objectives of the IMF. We are also referring to how that "strategic opacity" (a term that Raquel Gutiérrez Aguilar uses to characterize the current conflict and that we can also use to describe the language of financial speculation) is converted into a drastic reduction in our purchasing power, the value of our wages and subsidies, and the uncontrolled increase in prices and rates. The speed and vertigo of that "depreciation" of value is part of the terror (of the violence of money) and the disciplining that seeks to make us submissive through the fear that everything could be even worse. Financial terror holds hostage the desire for transformation: it produces a psychological terror that consists of forcing us to only want things to stop getting worse.

In this register, it is essential to historicize the link between public debt and the military dictatorship, as Bruno Nápoli, Celeste Perosino, and Walter Bosisio (2014) have researched in Argentina. Additionally, Pedro Biscay's (2015) work updating the relationship between finance, democracy, and human rights is essential. These authors show how the military dictatorship (1976–83), responsible for the disappearance, murder, and torture of 30,000 people, marks the beginning of the neo-liberalism that would develop over the following decades. The Financial Entities Law enacted in 1977 is a milestone for opening the way for financialization and it remains in effect today, since no democratic government has been able to overturn it. Additionally, it is necessary to recognize the structuring role played by foreign debt that also originated during the period of dictatorship.

But there is something else. When we speak of *financial terror* we are also referring to how finance (at the hands of banks and their subsidiary companies: from those offering "cash now" to credit cards, as well as other, more informal dynamics) have taken over household and family economies through popular indebtedness. Today, the financialization of everyday life forces the poorest sectors (and now not only those sectors) to go into debt to pay for food and medication and to finance the payment of basic services in installments with incredibly high interest rates. In other words, subsistence itself generates debt.

Financial terror, then, is a structure of obedience that operates over the day-to-day and time to come and forces us to take on the costs of structural adjustment in an individual and private way. But additionally it *normalizes* the fact that our lives are only sustainable through debt, in a type of *financialization of daily life* (Martin 2002).

Financial terror functions as an everyday "counter-revolution" in the sense that it operates on the same plane on which the feminist revolution forcefully unfolded, where feminism has led to crises in relations of submission and obedience, defying sexist violence and challenging the domestic sphere as one of seclusion.

DEBT AS A "COUNTER-REVOLUTION" OF EVERYDAY LIFE

Today, generalized indebtedness *pays off* the crisis so that each person confronts rate increases individually and must spend increasingly more time working for ever less money. Today, the very act of living "produces" debt. In that process, an "inverted" image appears of the very productivity of our labor power, of our vital *potencia*.[2]

Debt is a way of *managing the crisis*: nothing explodes but everything implodes. Inwards, in families, in households, in workplaces, in neighborhoods, financial obligation makes relationships become increasingly fragile and precarious due to the permanent pressure of debt. The structure of mass indebtedness that has existed for over a decade is what gives us clues to the current form taken by the crisis: as an individual responsibility, as an increase in so-called "domestic" violence, as a greater precarization of existence.

Indebtedness, we can say using Caffentzis's (2018) image, manages the "patience" of workers, of housewives, of students, of migrants, and others. The question about patience is the following: How long will we put up with the violent conditions that are necessary for capital to reproduce and valorize itself today? The subjective dimension that marks the limits of capital is a key element of mass indebtedness.

Today, it is the feminist movement, more than other forms of leftist politics, that is raising a dispute precisely over that "subjective" element: over the modes of disobedience, non-compliance, and refusal of contemporary dynamics of violence, which are intimately connected to exploitation and value extraction. Through the process of organizing the international feminist strike we have pushed this point, which is also strategic: rendering visible and connecting the non-recognized aspects of labor, rejecting the hierarchy between the productive and the reproductive, and constructing a shared horizon of struggles that reformulates the very notions of body, conflict, and territory.

THE WRITING ON THE BODY OF WOMEN

We take this phrase from Rita Segato (2013), in order to think about how the violence of the crisis is inscribed on the bodies of women, lesbians, trans people, and travestis today. We start from a concrete image: the pots that left the households and went onto the streets as impoverish-

2. In Spanish, there are two words for "power": "poder" and "potencia," which derive from the Latin "potestas" and "potentia" respectively. Here "poder" is identified with static, constituted power, while "potencia" has a dynamic, constituent dimension. Potencia defines our power to do, to be affected and to affect others, while "poder" refers to power over, a form of power based on the mechanism of representation that separates the bodies being represented from their own "potencia."

ment became more brutal. These *ollas populares*, literally "popular pots," are collectively prepared and freely distributed meals in public places, in plazas, on streets, in front of government buildings, that simultaneously address people's hunger and function as a form of protest, politicizing the crisis of reproduction.

In Argentina, Corina de Bonis, a primary school teacher, was kidnapped and tortured for protesting against school closures in the locality of Moreno, in the urban periphery of Buenos Aires in September 2018. The words "no more pots" were carved onto her stomach, on the same day that Teachers' Day was being celebrated in Argentina. It is a powerful scene of torture: they *literally* write the terror that they want to communicate on women's bodies. The assailants write on the body of the teacher in struggle, torturing her. It transmits a message: the same one that was already circulating through anonymous fliers that said that the next *olla* would be in the cemetery.

That is because the pots – and that practice of collective cooking and eating – in the street are seen from the position of power as the witches' cauldrons were earlier: spaces for meeting, nutrition, and conversation, where resistance is woven together, where a common body is manufactured as a spell against hunger, where people cook in opposition and conspire against their condemnation to poverty and resignation. Why do they literally write "no more pots" on that body? Because they are afraid of the pot. Because the pot destroys all the abstraction concealed by the words of financial terror: both the zero deficit and the immateriality of the stock markets are taken apart by the forcefulness of a pot that translates the implications of inflation and austerity in everyday life into a powerful and unobjectionable image.

In recent months, women started taking the pots out to the streets again (as they did in the roadblocks organized by the movements of unemployed workers before and after the crisis in 2001): a communitarian know-how emerges once again, the ability to collectivize what people have, and to foreground the defense of life as feminist politics. Taking the pots out onto the streets also means politicizing the domestic, as the feminist movement has long been doing: removing it from its enclosure, confinement, and solitude. The domestic becomes an open space on the street. That is the politicization of the crisis of reproduction.

To the crisis that grows at the rhythm of inflation, the austerity imposed by mass layoffs, and cuts to public policies, we can add the bankarization of food: "food" cards that can only be rung up in certain businesses and that today are unusable because of the "lack" of prices caused by the speculation carried out by some grocery stores. All of this is translated into hunger for millions of people. Today, that hunger is criminalized through the ongoing militarization of social conflict, using the specter of "looting" as a threat of repression, and the persecution of protests in the name of "security."

Several women from social organizations recount how they skip meals as a mode of self-adjustment in the face of food scarcity, so as to be better able to share it among their children. Technically, this is called "food insecurity." Politically, it shows how women put their bodies on the line in a differential way, against the crisis as well.

Financial speculation wages war against bodies on the street and the pots that resist. The pots that today are connected to the cauldrons from before. Pots become cauldrons. In Argentina, at the moment, social reproduction is in crisis in many neighborhoods and knowledges of the crisis are emerging. Confronted with this situation, the government doubles down on its wager: financial terror, terror in the style of task groups and psychological terror.

NEITHER VICTIMS NOR ENTREPRENEURS

It is not a coincidence that in October 2018, the Women20 met in Argentina: that is, the group of women that the G20 (the group of the 20 most powerful countries in the world) has organized to translate the feminist movement's agenda into a neoliberal register. It is not a coincidence that the summit was held in Argentina, known around the world for its massive and radical feminist movement. It is not a coincidence that one of the main proposals is for women's "financial inclusion" to make us all believe that we can be entrepreneurs if we manage to go into (even more!) debt. Here we see how the idea of "financial inclusion" seeks to cover up forms of financial exploitation, especially targeting women who are understood as "natural" entrepreneurs.

The "farce" of inclusion through finance supposes imposing the idea that becoming an entrepreneur of oneself is the ideal that we all aspire to and that the banks support. The entrepreneur complements the figure of the victim: the two positions of subjectivation proposed by a pink-washing neoliberalism. The feminist response is a refusal: *we are neither victims nor entrepreneurs.* The feminist response takes on strength thanks to another refusal: saying no to domestic confinement and the private and miserabilist management of the crisis.

The pots-cauldrons come out in opposition to the government of finance. The pots on the streets weave a politics of bodies in resistance, they light the collective fire against the inexistence that they try to condemn us to, and shout: "we are not afraid of them!"

FEMINIST INSUBORDINATION AND FASCIST NEOLIBERALISM

In his course titled *The Punitive Society* (2018 [1973]), Michel Foucault outlines an analogy between the appearance of the prison and the wage form: both are based on a system of equivalence in which time is the interchangeable unit. For this to be possible, it is necessary to conquer the power of time in an extractive sense. The wage and prison are connected as historically specific formulas for the extraction of time.

However, the wage functions by exploiting labor that has already taken place while prison exploits a time to come. In this sense, the prison form shows more similarities with the debt-form if we think of it as another mechanism for value extraction. Both prison and debt work over future time. But if prison fixates and disciplines, debt puts us to work, mobilizes, commands, as we already noted.

Debt, if we understand it historically as a response to a specific sequence of struggles, is also a mechanism for the extraction of life time and labor time, reconfiguring the very notion of class. Our hypothesis is that debt functions retroactively as a machine of capture of social inventions aimed at the self-management of work and the politicization of social reproduction. In the case of Argentina (which can be expanded to Latin America as a whole), debt functions *backwards*, functioning to exploit and contain the excess of popular productivity, which feminism has radicalized. Social protests provide us with the interpretative coordinates for understanding how debt has organized its expansion as an apparatus of class government. However, this also requires thinking about what we classify as conflicts, capable of challenging the valorization of capital. We see the repetition of a philosophical and nostalgic mansplaining that only recognizes revolution (of course, defeated) in the 1970s (see, for example, Lazzarato 2020). The feminist reading of debt is precisely the opposite: it recognizes the massiveness and radicality of the feminist revolution that we are witnessing today.

Starting from there, we are interested in thinking about how debt currently anticipates a temporality of capture and how it is launched to control future capacity for invention, in response to concrete threats to capital accumulation. Here we see a specific form of interconnection between the neoliberal project that financializes ever more areas of life and fascism that today focuses on disciplining indeterminacy in desires, practices, and modes of life.

It is along this line that we interpret the growing call to include "financial education" as part of the complementary curriculum in schools, as well as the recent project to offer loans to young people who "neither work nor study" and that enter the gendarme school (meanwhile sexual education in schools is attacked as "gender ideology").

The relationship with the future temporality supposed by the financial obligation is a fundamental element for understanding the importance acquired both by the legal dimension of the obligation as well as of the moralization of default, especially targeting young people. The dispute is over the development of subjectivities, over control of social inventions in the future.

We see in action what Foucault understood as a constant transcription between morality and law, or, in other words, the scenes in which the dispute over moral conditionings materializes, over which the law later operates. Therefore, it is increasingly clear how the financial recolonization of our continent proposed by fascist neoliberalism simultaneously demands the production of young people who are indebted and disciplined by the mandate of the heteropatriarchal family.

COUNTER-OFFENSIVE

Green Bills Against the Green Tide

In May 2018, on the same day that the Lebacs expired (the Central Bank's notes that they used for financial speculation to try to attract foreign dollars in exchange for high interest rates for bonds in pesos), the *ollas populares* were steaming in front of the Central Bank. The day had been named "Black Tuesday" in advance, anticipating that the sale of bonds would crown a week of bank runs and a non-stop increase in the value of the dollar. Along with the *ollas populares*, activists from grassroots organizations had previously read out manifestos inside two financial institutions, the Bank of the Province of Buenos Aires and the Stock Exchange.

In June 2018, the day after the first massive vigil as the lower house of Congress debated the law of legal, safe, and free abortion, the state sought to *oppose the green tide with the run on green bills:* that is, print over the leap in the price of the dollar the day after the feminist victory. June 13 was the day of the "green tide," with one million people camping out all night around the Congress building in support of abortion rights and waving the green handkerchiefs symbolizing that campaign, and in the early morning the lower house approved the bill in favor of the legalization of abortion.[3] That same morning, while we feminists were still in the streets, the news of the "green tide" competed with the "green run" referring to the uncontrollable increase in the value of the dollar. So the image is that of an opposition between "greens" (the green of the abortion campaign and the green dollar) and the opposition between a million bodies taking to the streets and the decorporealization of monetary speculation. These events are not disconnected. Rather, we can analyze a competition of forces that takes place there: as if they were seeking to crush the bodies dyed green, in support of abortion rights, on the street with the decorporealized green of financial speculation.

Don't Mess with My Children

There can be no debt without an economy of obedience that sustains it. Debt is also a differentiated moralization over the lives and desires of women and feminized bodies. What happens when workers' morality is not produced in the factory and through its habits of discipline tied to repetitive mechanical labor? How does debt function as an apparatus of moralization when it replaces that factory discipline? How does moralization operate over a flexible, precarious, and, from a certain point of view, undisciplined, labor force? *What does debt, as an economy of obedience, have to do with the crisis of the heteropatriarchal family?*

Melinda Cooper (2017) dismantles the widespread idea that neoliberalism is an amoral or even anti-normative regime, demonstrating the affinity that exists between the promotion of the heterosexual family as the basic unit of social life and the reification of the traditional role of

---

3.   In August of 2018, the bill for legal, free, and safe abortion was defeated in Argentina's Senate but was ultimately passed in December 2020.

women in that structure and the need for women to take on increasingly more tasks for reproduction of life in the face of the privatization of social services. Targeted social assistance (the preferred form of neoliberal state intervention) also reinforces a hierarchy of merit in relation to women's obligation according to their roles in the patriarchal family: having children, caring for them, sending them to school, vaccinating them. Thus, the importance of what we have referred to as the *politicization of reproduction* that unfolds in the *ollas* on the street and in other community activities becomes clear. Those practices are able to challenge the enclosure of reproductive tasks, taking them outside of the heteronormative family.

Therefore, we want to propose a connection between debt as a moralizing organization of life and the slogan "Don't mess with my children" (#ConMisHijosNoTeMetas), taken up by conservative groups across Latin America, with church backing, to oppose any instance of feminist perspectives, comprehensive sexual education, or even the word "gender" in state policy or school curriculum. As one of the interviews in this book recounts, debt is introduced at an increasingly early age, for 18-year-old boys and girls seeking their first insertion into the labor market. Debt is proposed as a "structure" of obligation for those incipient and precarious labor trajectories. While employment is intermittent, debt is long term. Thus, it functions as continuity in terms of its obligation in the face of the discontinuity of income, making those incomes (that are increasingly used to make interest and installment payments) even more fragile, and as a growing blackmail forcing people to accept any type of working conditions.

What type of *moral education* is necessary for indebted and precarious youth? It is not a coincidence that the government tries to impose *financial education in schools at the same time as it rejects the implementation of Comprehensive Sexual Education (ESI)*, which is translated into budget cuts, outsourcing it to religious NGOs, and restricting it to a preventative norm. Sexual education is limited and redirected to constrict its ability to open imaginaries and to legitimate the practice of other relations and desires beyond the heteronormative family. Fighting it in the name of "Don't Mess with My Children" (as conservatives are doing in Argentina and in several countries of the region under the so-called fight against "gender ideology") is a "crusade" for the remoralization of youth, which the state seeks to complement with early "financial education."

Schools have been an important element of resistance in Brazil in recent years. Students carried out massive and powerful occupations in 2015 and have since been the target of backlash, accused today of spreading "gender ideology" as an attempt to discipline them. It is in the educational establishments ranging from elementary school to universities that education with a feminist perspective is criminalized because it opens a sort of elaboration of desire that suspends the mandate of the heteropatriarchal family as the only possible destiny for the lives of adolescents and children, politicizing young people in a way that is persecuted across the continent. This is also notable in Chile, where schools have been occupied by police forces (literally permanently occupying the rooftops of emblematic buildings) in another extreme case of this regional witch hunt. This attack also criminalizes the insurgency of the new generations that led the feminist uprising in May 2018, but that comes from a continuum of forces of the student movement that has been mobilizing for years. Today, along with the demand for free public education to be able to go to university debt free, they also demand non-sexist education.

As moral apparatuses, the family and finance make up a joint machine. Therefore, the religious counter-offensive directed against the feminist tide is simultaneously an economic counter-offensive. Finance and religion *structure complementary economies of obedience.*

What we see in this scene is how young people's bodies are a battlefield over which capital seeks to expand the frontiers of its valorization, turning them into workers who are obedient to precarization, debt, and the nuclear family (even if it is violent and imploded). Finance is allowed to mess with children from a young age.

GENTLEMEN'S AGREEMENT

We speak of a "gentlemen's agreement" to characterize the pact that Macri's government established during its last year in office (2019), before its electoral defeat, with the food company monopolies. The image, however, came from the finance minister himself when he announced that prices would be frozen for six months for 60 basic goods due to the inflationary crisis. He was trying to explain that the agreement didn't need any institutional reinsurance or written commitment since he trusted in the masculine camaraderie between business leaders and state officials. We believe that this formula of a "gentlemen's agreement" speaks to us about something broader: a patriarchal proposal to resolve the crisis. What does that mean?

1. "Resolving" the crisis by trusting in monopolies.

The government sought to encapsulate the crisis that, as we know, directly affects everyday life – we are talking about "basic foodstuffs!" – in an agreement between the same gentlemen who are responsible (as a political class and business leaders) for the concentration of food production through dispossessing family producers and strangling other small-scale economies, and therefore, for the uncontrolled rise in prices. This has exponential effects in the face of the already consolidated financialization of food provisioning (through the compulsory individual bankarization achieved a decade ago through the food cards) and the expansion of agribusiness as a productive model.

2. "Resolving" the crisis with more debt.

Another one of the proclamations in 2019 to "relieve" the crisis was a new shock of loans that are granted through the public agency responsible for distributing benefits to retirees and other beneficiaries of social assistance. The goal was to deepen financial exploitation of the sectors with the fewest resources, inserting debt into each household as an apparatus of future impoverishment.

3. "Resolving" the crisis by painting the financial problem as a debate between technical experts.

Financial speculation is unthinkable without political speculation. Both are machines of "waiting," of playing with our futures: during a run on the dollar, the headlines of the *Clarín* (the newspaper with the most readership in Argentina) assured the public that the Central Bank "is trying to control the run by selling futures." The financial problem, when it is narrated as a technical problem, is delegated to a negotiation between gentlemen. It is a twofold depoliticization: you cannot intervene "now" and the everyday consequences of finance are denied. Political speculation follows the rhythm of financial speculation and financial speculation leads to political speculation.

THE PATRIARCHY HAS MY MISSING CONTRIBUTIONS

Pension reform is one of the key demands expressed by the IMF as part of the austerity policies imposed by debt. We understand it as a *punitive reform of social rights*. The IMF proposed, as in several other countries, a cut to retirement rights, particularly the "pension moratorium" for "housewives," a name that was used to speak of pension rights for those who carried out unpaid or badly paid work their whole lives and whose employers were not responsible for making contributions for them. The feminist movement has framed it as a punishment-cut: an attempt at discipline that is inseparable from economic adjustment.

The joint feminist and labor movement mobilization, which rendered visible and placed value on reproductive, care, and attention labor, while also denouncing the wage gap sustained by the sexual division of labor, was at the forefront of the rejection of the government's proclamation. With the slogan-concept "All women are workers," the inter-union, a historic feminist alliance between women unionists of all the union federations in Argentina, broadened both what is understood by work as well as the capacity to dispute remuneration and recognition of historically non-paid or badly paid feminized labor.

The "benefit" of the pension moratorium is a question that should at least be problematized: rights are only accessed through debt. With the moratorium, contributions, which should be the responsibility of the state and employers, are "bought" individually. But along with privately assuming the contributions were not made by those who benefited from their labor, those women workers are also restricted by a socioeconomic report that "certifies" their poverty. The government, through this filter, has reduced the population of women able to access the moratorium using the criterion that they did not demonstrate enough "vulnerability."

Again, we see a patriarchal punishment in action against the possibility of living an old age beyond austerity and domestic confinement. And once again, opposition mobilizations forced the government to finally back down. The performance of vulnerability is opposed to the recognition of a work history that is now reinterpreted and valorized in the register of rights and the demand to enjoy old age as autonomy and not as years of being treated as waste, unproductive and miserable.

Associating the right to retirement of so-called "housewives" with the certificate of vulnerability and poverty is a way of normalizing gender hierarchies and, at the same time, of fueling the rising conservatism that proposes a "return to the home" for all of those women who have rebelled against the family mandate, no matter what generation they belong to. A statistic from the Centro de Estudios Distributivos, Laborales y Sociales (CEDLAS) of the University of La Plata (Berniell et al. 2017) shows what those retirement payments meant in the life of many women: according to that study, the probability of divorce/separation rose 2.6 percent, which is translated into an 18 percent increase in the number of divorces for couples older than sixty.

Then, the punitive reform of social rights includes a series of mechanisms: the translation of rights into terms of individual debt and the moralization of access to them through the certification of poverty. Meanwhile, the government publicized new loans that use the retirement benefits and social assistance as guarantees, after child poverty increased to 51.7 percent in 2018. This confirms two premises of "public policy": that the retirement benefits are not enough to live off and the way to make up what is missing is through debt. Retirement benefits do not play the role of even guaranteeing subsistence, but they do give the state's seal of approval to financial capital to invade the everyday life of the poorest people.

The classic slogan "from work to home" stamped the route of the disciplined worker without "distractions" between the factory and the family-home. What that trajectory made clear was the sexual division of labor: one place for work, another for rest. Of course the "subject" of movement, who went from one place to another, was male, synonymous with the worker. The feminist movement overturned and tore apart that image and, above all, the meaning of those "locations" based on an understanding of work from the male point of view: that which is done outside the home and from which the home functions as a space of refuge and rest for the male breadwinner, under the housewife's obligation to keep the home shiny clean. Feminists in the 1970s started to explain that the assembly line starts in the kitchen and that women's bodies are the "factories" that create the labor force and, therefore, are subjected to all types of disciplining to promote their "productivity," in other words, forced maternity.

Today, the alliance between the union movement and feminism – empowered in the political exercise of the feminist strikes over the last four years – has enabled unions to propose, under the slogan "Not One Retired Woman Less," recognition of "non-recognized" labor as a priority on the labor agenda. "They have always separated us: those women who work in factories, in offices, in schools, and in the home. It has been very difficult to create a common terrain, due to economic, social, and generational differences. But now the feminist movement is doing it," Silvia Federici said last year, in a meeting with women activists from all the union federations in the historical headquarters of the Federacion Gráfica Bonaerense on Paseo Colón Avenue, a place filled with mythical significance for the labor movement.

In this way, the feminist movement has constructed a general reading of labor because it is able to analyze, due to its historically *partial* position as devalued subjects, how the very idea of *normal* work has imploded. Of course, that normal labor that is presented as the hegemonic image of a waged, male, cis-heterosexual, formal job persists in the general imaginary or even as an ideal. But to the extent that it has become scarce, that ideal can function in a reactionary way: those who have that type of job are limited to perceiving themselves as the privileged who are in danger and who need to defend themselves from the tide of precarious workers, the unemployed, migrants, and informal workers. Much of union politics is also currently forced to act as if it were "defending privileges" and therefore in a reactionary register in the face of the generalized crisis and particularly in regards to the multiplication of labor.

The feminist-union alliance is fundamental because it proposes an agenda that recognizes and responds to the changes in the composition of labor and that is capable of inverting the reactionary hierarchy. Instead of setting its sole horizon as the defense of formal work, it starts by recognizing all the tasks that are not identified as labor. Thus, it produces a common field of action among those who are historically not recognized as value producers: women, sexual dissidents, migrants, popular economy workers, among others. The transversal composition of the feminist movement of recent years has opened up the imaginary for thinking about, for example, what a pension moratorium would look like that took into account the specificity of the life expectancy of the trans-travesti population, which currently does not reach forty years of age.

The reactionary mode of understanding the world of work (in which some workers pose a threat to others) is combined with neoliberal forms of promoting micro-entrepreneurship as a formula for "overcoming" the crisis of formal waged labor. Becoming an entrepreneur and going into debt seem to be opposed to the conservative and nostalgic rhetoric of stable employment. But what we see is a practical alliance between neoliberalism and conservatism. Neoliberalism becomes stronger where the conservative pro-family and cis-heteronormative mandate privatizes the consequences of austerity: within domestic enclosure, under the language of individual responsibility and family indebtedness.

For all these reasons, the *potencia* of the *current feminist diagnosis* of the map of labor lies in making a *non-fascist reading* of the end of a certain paradigm of inclusion through waged employment and in deploying other images of what we call work and other formulas for its recognition and retribution.

The transversality of the feminist movement finds a very important ally in the union component, both in terms of mobilization and in terms of its massiveness and impact. And, in turn, it achieves a capacity of joint force that transforms the question of union "unity" because it *overflows a traditional definition of who are considered workers.* For example, there has been inter-union recognition of women workers of the popular economy and of non-unionized workers, housewives, and retired women.

When the union recognizes the production of value in reproductive, communitarian, neighborhood, and precarious tasks, the union limit ceases to be a "fence" that confines work as *exclusively* belonging to formal workers. This gesture also shines light on other tasks that are covered up and that the wage and precarization also exploit.

Therefore, when we gender the historical chant "Workers' unity, and if you don't like it fuck off!" by specifying women workers, we are identifying a unity that cannot be consecrated within the framework of sexist hierarchies. The movement's force within unions actually denounces the fact that the unity that subordinated women workers was achieved through disciplining and obedience. On the other hand, by broadening the notion of women workers – because all women are workers – that unity becomes a force of *transversality*: it is composed of tasks and jobs that unions did not historically recognize as work and that is projected in the historic vindication: "Not One Retired Woman Less."

DEBT AND URBAN DEVELOPMENT IN THE CITY OF BUENOS AIRES

We see a specific mode of debt in operation in relation to real estate speculation. As Raquel Rolnik (2018) says, we are faced with a "colonization of land and housing in the era of finance." To explore this question, we can look at *Villa 31*, one of the *villas* (slums) located in the center of the city of Buenos Aires, which is currently the object of the most violent process of urban development of recent times.

It is not a coincidence: it is a strategic area for port logistics and land speculation due to its location. It was the neighborhood's feminist assembly that set out to unmask and resist the process of urban development in one of the areas of the city most coveted by the city government and real estate capital, which began the project by establishing a McDonald's and Santander Bank there. In turn, the Interamerican Development Bank plans to build their headquarters there in a "building-bridge" that would unite the slum with the elite neighborhood of Recoleta.

There is a lot at stake here: the city government wants to sell plots of land in the *villa* to pay off its debt with international credit organizations. Feminists made a precise call for an assembly about "Urban development in a feminist register, in opposition to debt and gender mandates." They elaborated a map of the forms of resistance to the advance of real estate business in the *villa*, in which feminist collectives feature prominently, and discussed how this process is related to public and private indebtedness and the gender mandates used to select beneficiaries for subsidized housing. The debate in the assembly was divided into two themes, "Precarities and debt" and "Feminist territorial organization," which together form a complete agenda for action, a cartography of what is to be done with a feminist grammar.

The new, recently constructed public housing is distributed through loans. That is, first you have to abandon the land and your own house, built with much effort through self-managed labor, to become the "virtual" owner of another dwelling that you have access to through a commitment to make a monthly loan payment. Along with these payments, there are two additional elements that further complicate your everyday economy. First, you must start paying for services (gas, electricity, etc.) in dollarized rates, because the communitarian "connections," which were victories of earlier social mobilizations for free or affordable services, are lost. And, second, you also lose the possibility to work and/or operate a business where you work because of the very design of the new houses.

The new housing is not prepared for people to continue labor activities ranging from carpentry and mechanics to blacksmithing, laundry, and small retail businesses. "Indebted and without work: how do they expect us to pay? It is clear that they prefer that we don't pay so that they can keep the titles of 'our' houses," says one of the inhabitants. Several of the residents also recount how those who resist the urban development plan have had their electricity cut off and trash thrown at their door, in order to pressure and harass them.

The deeds already incorporate a "legal" form of eviction in the event of entering into arrears on payments, which is very likely to happen in the current difficult economic situation. This also applies for the non-payment of services (water, electricity, gas). In other words, everything puts the ownership of the home at risk and everything is prepared to produce an eviction through legal means, that is, provoked and mediated by the debt mechanism.

But financialization is not limited to the titling of the houses based on debt; the bill approved in the City Legislature also incorporates the possibility of selling the titles of the mortgage debts to third parties. In this way, after the residents are "produced" as debtors of banks or investment funds, they will have no other "option" but to sell their houses and land. Supposedly the solution is to turn them into property owners: in practice this functions as a moment that enables dispossession. The government, in turn, argues that the land "liberated" by evictions will be sold to pay off the debt with international credit agencies that was taken out to remodel the wealthy parts of the city, thus shaping a circuit that links violence, public debt, private debt, and expulsions in a perfect circle.

The feminist perspective on urbanization is not limited to denouncing the process of titling based on debt, but goes further. It also problematizes and denounces the fact that the property deeds that the government promises are distributed based on cis-heterosexist criteria and that they act as a way of remoralizing the lives of women, lesbians, travestis, and trans persons. In fact, the deeds are given to men or women who live in heterosexual families with children. Thus, the government's way of classifying subjects to determine who deserves housing produces a system of punishment for those lives outside of the heterosexual family. In response, organized feminist resistance maps, denounces, and above all, stays alert.

FROM FINANCE TO BODIES

After Macri's forceful electoral defeat in late 2019, politics continued by other means, more precisely through the currency war. This is what we have been calling financial terrorism, which only accelerated in the electoral moment.

Financial terrorism has many methods: the threatening discourse about the ever imminent catastrophe, the uncontrolled trajectory of interest rates, the caste of bondholders, the technical language of experts, the faceless currency runs that nobody takes responsibility for, the generalized indebtedness.

Currency expresses social relations, that is, relations of force. It was never more clear that, as was demonstrated in the voracity of the devaluation the day immediately following the elections,[4] a civil war is played out in currency value (as Marx said). There is nothing abstract or enigmatic about the rise in the dollar: there are disputes against specific bodies.

The currency war is a key element of global politics and local politics: a planetary war of positions is unleashed between the yuan and the dollar. In Argentina we are facing a covert dollarization: what we managed to defeat in the streets in December 2001 (at that time the government was talking about taking the Ecuadorian path of officially dollarizing the economy) has now been established through other means (dollarization of service rates, the real estate market, food, and medicine). The inflationary crisis and the phantom of shortages of sensitive products seem to raise a false analogy with that era at the turn of the century and, even with the hyperinflation of the 1980s. However, since there is no widespread looting, which is what we associate with out of control prices in our historical memory, it feels "as if" the crisis was not fully unleashed or that it was impossible to measure its true impact.

Financial terror is successful. A financial containment from below that sustains mass impoverishment (and its psychological terror) is being established through the constant refinancing of debt with more debt for purchasing basic products and paying utilities and services.

Going from finance to bodies, in a move that removes the violence of currency from the sky of abstraction, is a methodology developed by the feminist movement that becomes essential for analyzing the current landscape.

Let's take a concrete example. The LELIQ (the Central Bank's liquidity bills) imply a political operation: they are supported by private savings

4. Following incumbent president Mauricio Macri's resounding defeat at the polls, the value of the peso plunged, losing 25 percent of its value within three days.

and the mass of wages, subsidies, and pensions. Banks are using the money of workers, savers, and beneficiaries of social rights to speculate and obtain the world's highest interest rates in minimal installments (Blanco et al. 2018). Thus, this financial instrument is turned into a time bomb that encapsulates, postpones, and obscures the conflict that it contains.

Therefore, the problem of the LELIQ cannot only be understood as a technical problem to be "dismantled"; they are a political-financial operation that ties the fate of savers, workers, and welfare beneficiaries to that of banks. It is this type of confiscation of political capacity that makes up the terrorism of the so-called markets and consequent justification for bailing out the banks.

Over the course of those years, popular and feminist mobilizations constructed a forceful veto power to Macri's economic program, which was then also expressed at the ballot boxes. The financial extortion – and debt as a privatized way of confronting poverty – attempts to also expropriate that capacity of veto and strengthen disciplining through the most violent and rapid devaluation. This has also played out as a dispute within the institutional field, in terms of who makes up new government.

The fact that a government that promoted public and private debt as a mode of expropriation and impoverishment was massively rejected at the ballot boxes raises the question of how to bring conflict into what is presented as a "market decision," how to confront finance when it becomes a capillary terror.

It is not enough to confront finance with the language of speculation and waiting: that is its language. Today, we see how delegating problems to technical expertise or future negotiation gives finance the monopoly over "producing" crisis as a preferred political mechanism of extortion and blackmail. It is also impossible to reduce the debate to terms of national sovereignty due to finance's global dimension. Confronted with that geopolitics, the force of the streets and its capacity to be translated into an electoral mandate is crucial. We need to simultaneously discuss and put into practice non-usurious systems of loans (other interest rates), forms of household debt relief (proposals for alternative financing and forgiving existing debts), and alternative currencies (with local circuits and material referenciality) that reduce the damage of inflation. We need to denounce and confront dispossession, looting, and financial violence in the here and now.

VOLUNTARY TERMINATION OF DEBT

The inauguration of the new government of Alberto Fernández (December 2019) was marked by two issues: the impact of feminism in the debates and the discussion about the "renegotiation" of the foreign debt, which is generally considered to be "unpayable." We propose a slogan that links the demand for the Voluntary Termination of Pregnancy (the multitudinous feminist demand of the "green tide") with that of debt: Voluntary Termination of Debt. It is a synthesizing formula to propose the idea that along with debt relief, policies are needed that recognize the value of domestic labor and that would directly make us "creditors" of a wealth that we have *already* created for free. We say that it is time for reappropriation, for a legal termination of debt.

Today, the effects of debt fall on areas that are sensitive and politically delicate because they directly exploit the capacity for social reproduction: household debt and food prices, both increasing uncontrollably at the inflationary rhythm of recent years.

As one of the first emergency measures, the new government launched a program called "Argentina against Hunger." We should note that in Argentina, the world's fourth largest soy producer, 48 percent of children live in poverty.

The program consists of distributing food cards that would seek to reach two million people. The Minister of Social Development, Daniel Arroyo, in charge of the measure, used a crude empirical fact to explain why the program was being implemented through a system of food cards and not by directly distributing cash: any cash that families would receive would go immediately to paying (formal or informal) debt as those families are completely indebted. The conclusion is obvious. The ability to guarantee food access today is determined by a household's debt, which literally functions as a parasite on all other types of income: from retirement payments to state benefits, especially the Universal Child Allowance, from regular wages to intermittent payments from odd jobs.

This link between debt and food is key because it takes the destructive effects of precarity to their extreme: going into debt to eat, first; and, on the other end of the chain, drowning in debts to be able to produce food in the popular economies; and finally, the monopolistic bottleneck of supermarkets. Thus we see how the diagnosis of the financial colonization of our territories is much broader than the legacy of the foreign debt, although it is directly related to it. The external debt spills over, as a capillary system of indebtedness into household debt, and is reinforced by the loss of purchasing power and cuts to public services. It is an explosive combination. Or, in other words, it only feeds more debt.

The struggles of small-scale agricultural producers, the workers of the land, have transformed how public policies for fighting hunger are designed in Argentina. Thanks to them, family and peasant agriculture and its circuit of markets directly linking producers to consumers are beginning to be included in ways of providing quality food. Rosalía Pellegrini from the Unión de Trabajadores de la Tierra (Union of Workers of the Land) claims: "For us, this was accomplished through the *verduda-zos*," referring to the political actions in which they unloaded enormous quantities of vegetables in plazas and handed them out for free, denouncing how inflation was making life unsustainable both for small farmers and consumers.

Here the lines of the challenge are drawn. On one side, the food cards are an attempt to institutionalize the *feriazos*, those protests distributing free food, and to recognize the social movement's diagnosis of the issue of hunger. On the other hand, the inherited indebtedness and the system of bankarization creates an unreal equivalence between transnational supermarket chains and popular markets.

The conditions of production and hyper-exploitation of family agriculture today point to two structural problems: the limits imposed by not having access to land (and therefore the need to pay expensive leases) and, second, the unrecognized labor of campesina women. A quadruple knot narrows the possibilities and complicates the picture: the tax question, land ownership, the financialization of food, and the quantity of unrecognized and historically devalued feminized labor that functions, in fact, as a variable for lowering costs. Rosalía adds, "Our food is subsidized by our self-exploitation, we go into debt to be able to compete in a dependent production model."

HUNGER AND GENDER MANDATES

There is another aspect to the public declarations announcing the implementation of the food card: the insistent interpellation of maternal responsibility for feeding children, even when the card is targeted at mothers or fathers. The responsibilization of hyper-exploited mothers risks re-establishing forms of patriarchal meritocracy in social assistance.

A feminist perspective, on the other hand, demands that social policies not be used to naturalize a gender mandate in a context of extreme crisis.

Cuts to public services and the dollarization of rates and food during Mauricio Macri's government shifted the "costs" of social reproduction onto the family. Now it is necessary to re-establish public services so that responsibilities for food and care no longer fall on the family. The feminist movement has shown the violent limitations of the family when it is reduced to its heteropatriarchal norm and, in turn, has valued communitarian networks for their capacity to produce social relations and institutional mediation. "The food card is an important measure in the face of the extreme needs of our compañeras but it does not replace the food ration that is handed out in each neighborhood soup kitchen, where they carry out *ollas populares*, and it is that communitarian labor that we demand be recognized," says Jackie Flores from the Movement of Excluded Workers and the Union of Popular Economy Workers (UTEP).

THE DEBT OF CARE

Over these years, there has been a growing recognition of reproductive labor (including, but not limited to, care work). An enormous quantity of tasks have been identified and mapped that are productive of value, but were politically subordinated and hidden in the basements of everyday life. The feminist movement has vindicated these labors as politically productive, challenging their condemnation to be disregarded, free, badly paid, and compulsory.

The heart of the battle lies in delinking care from gender mandates that naturalize that labor and use biology to associate it with women in terms of a moral obligation. It is not a cultural battle, but strictly a political one. For example, we remember when, during an assembly, compañeras from union organizations shared that when parental leave had been offered to fathers they did not want to take it, showing that recognition and rights require a certain type of political order to become effective.

Here a historical debate about wages for care work comes into play: their significance, how to measure them, and their capacity to challenge the sexual division of labor. We are faced with an important challenge: we must not allow the wage that remunerates care work to get stuck in the lowest rungs of the wage ladder. That would confirm a hierarchy of tasks that would make it impossible for that wage to function as an antidote to precarization.

Speaking of care also allows us to understand how precarization functions in general in the current moment. The free, non-recognized, subordinated, intermittent, and at the same time constant, dimension of reproductive labor today allows us to analyze the components that accelerate processes of precarization. It allows us to understand the forms of intensive exploitation of affective infrastructure and, in turn, the extensive expansion of the working day in domestic space. It allows us to comprehend forms of migrant labor and new hierarchies in freelance work. In turn, it illuminates how availability and the ability to manage overlapping tasks are the primary subjective resource employed every day in childcare, as well as a contemporary requirement of service work.

Paying attention to prices, making daily adjustments to make incomes stretch further, and inventing more work are now everyday scenes that strain that logic of care as precarization escalates. The Uber driver accompanied by her child is no longer an exception, nor is the textile worker who has to leave her children, between the ages of three and seven, alone while she sews because she cannot get a spot in the public day care centers.

A FEMINIST ANALYSIS OF INFLATION

There is a political battle over what causes inflation. Different authors have contributed elements that enable us to elaborate a feminist analysis of inflation, the mechanism that forces us to take out debt at an accelerated rate.

Historically conservative arguments, which characterized inflation as an illness or moral ill of the economy, are added to monetarist explanations of inflation, which focus on the emission of currency. In other words, it is not only about technical and economic explanations, but is directly related to expectations of how to live, consume, and work. Thus argued the famous Harvard sociologist Daniel Bell who identified the breakdown of the domestic order as the main cause of inflation in the United States in the 1970s. So did Paul Volcker, Chair of the US Federal Reserve from 1979 to 1987, known for his proposal to discipline the working class as a method for combating inflation, establishing the issue as a "moral question."

Melinda Cooper's analysis of these explanations, as she studies why both neoliberals and conservatives raged against a low budget program aimed at assisting African American single mothers, provides a fundamental clue: that subsidy highlighted how its beneficiaries disobeyed moral expectations. Those African American single mothers produced an image that did not fit the Fordist family portrait. That is, from a conservative perspective, those who received assistance were being "rewarded" for their decision to have children outside of heteronormative cohabitation and inflation *reflected* the inflation of expectations of how to live their lives, without a mandatory requirement to work.

Then, conservatives take the classic neoliberal argument that inflation is due to "excess" public spending and wage increases due to union power, and add another twist: inflation marks a qualitative displacement of what is desired. More recently, both arguments have aligned decisively.

In our context, how can we discuss inflation in a way that deconstructs the conservative image of social spending, similar to that of the outgoing government, that imposes a moral mandate on and judges women from popular sectors for their possible spending, at the same time as it excuses the local and international financial elite responsible for the capital flight of nine out of every ten dollars of the national debt?

If there are relations that express rejection or flight from the family contract, becoming debtors is – as Silvia Federici argues – a change in the form of exploitation that leads to another question: How are people disciplined and punished outside of the wage relation and outside of marriage? Punitive reforms of social rights (as we argued in relation to the pension moratorium) seek to invent apparatuses to create a patriarchal meritocracy outside of the wage and outside of marriage.

HOW TO DISOBEY FINANCE?

We are interested in a feminist economics that involves a redefinition, based on diverse and dissident bodies, of what is considered labor and expropriation, of communitarian and feminized modes of doing in which popular, migrant, domestic, and precarious economies are disputed today. This feminist economics opens up a line of investigation about finance as a war against our autonomy (Gago 2018). We use that to redefine what disobedience means in practice and, thus, to establish limits to neoliberal capitalism's appropriation of our forms of life and desire.

We said that the feminist gesture in response to debt ultimately involves weaving together a refusal. The feminist strike has taken this question seriously by highlighting the connection between life, the feminization of labor, and financial exploitation. In other words: how do you carry out strikes and sabotage against finance? There are several practices that serve as a disobedient archive of "not paying." Here we will comment on a few that seem inspiring to us.

In 1994, in Mexico, after a brutal devaluation of the Mexican peso in respect to the dollar caused inflation to increase to the point that it was impossible to pay off personal loans and dollarized mortgage payments, 30 percent of indebted people fell into bankruptcy. Activists from the movement known as "El Barzón" coined the slogan "I owe, I won't deny it, but I'll pay what is fair" to place the responsibility on the government and the banks for the increase in their debts (Caffentzis 2013). The movement rapidly expanded throughout the country and forced the government to come to the aid of debtors.

In the heat of the Zapatista uprising and the recently implemented NAFTA, one of the first movements denouncing how the financial system abused and dispossessed small producers emerged. That denunciation inspired a wave of disobedience by debtors that expanded and emphasized how small peasant economies and household economies were being suffocated, and pointed out the connection between those debts and the pressure exercised by the debt of nation states.

In 2001, a debtors' movement rose up in Bolivia, during the government of Hugo Banzer. Debtors occupied the Superintendent of Banks, the Episcopal Conference, and the Ombudsman's Office, armed with dynamite. Oscar Guisoni (2012) recounted,

> The majority of those debtors are poor Indigenous people from the interior of the country, that have taken out loans from financial NGOs or private banks, with interest rates of over 40% annually, plus added strange and costly commissions, criminal charges for late payment, and a dozen more charges, that take the costs of small loans to an accumulated interest that in some cases reaches over 120%.

In this "Plan to Dynamite Debt," as the journalist wrote, one of the main goals was to burn all the debt records. Women organized as a Movement of Indebted Women and played an important leadership role in denouncing banking usury.

This "business of poverty" is detailed in the book by Graciela Toro (2010) that we referenced earlier, published by Mujeres Creando, which emphasizes something that seems fundamental to us, especially in Latin

America: the organic relationship between structural adjustment and microcredit, the state's complicit role in usury, the role of international cooperation, and the link between debt and migrants as "the exiles of neoliberalism" (Galindo 2004).

Following the collapse of the financial bubble provoked by the real estate boom in Spain, in February 2009, the Platform for People Affected by Mortgages (PAH) emerged. That movement remains active today and has continuously denounced real estate speculation and how banks profit from mortgages, with the state's support. They have carried out collective practices and direct action to stop evictions, functioning in many points across the country as decentralized groups. They have also highlighted the importance of the migrant and feminized composition of their organizers.

This movement has affirmed that the real estate oligopoly is what sustains accumulation by dispossession. With hashtags such as #WeAreStaying and #WeWillNotLeave, they denounce both real estate speculation under the financial impulse of loans that become unpayable as well as the increase in rents. They point to investment funds and large property owners as those directly responsible for the "expulsions," referring to financial entities, owners of multiple properties, and vulture funds.

Inaugurating the Occupy Wall Street movement in 2012, different activists gathered in front of the New York Stock Exchange and camped in Zuccotti Park. There the slogan emerged "We are the 99%," referring to a majority united by subjugation to debt that benefits the 1 percent of the world's wealthiest people. There, a working group – Strike Debt – produced a manual of financial disobedience called "The Debt Resistors' Operation Manual," taking up the notion of the strike in its twofold meaning: to go on strike and to strike against. They also organized debtors' assemblies and launched the "Rolling Jubilee" project that consisted of collectively buying students' debt at reduced prices to pay it and liberate them.

Burning debt, closing abusive loan businesses, denouncing mechanisms of extortion, and practicing tactics of collective debt relief were some of the points that structured a fight against finance's power of blackmail. They state it clearly in phrases that become slogans:

To the financial establishment of the world, we have only one thing to say: We owe you nothing. To our friends, our families, our communities, to humanity and to the natural world that makes our lives possible, we owe you everything. Every dollar we take from a fraudulent subprime mortgage speculator, every dollar we withhold from the collection agency is a tiny piece of our own lives and freedom that we can give back to our communities, to those we love and we respect. These are acts of debt resistance, which come in many other forms as well: fighting for free education and healthcare, defending a foreclosed home, demanding higher wages and providing mutual aid. (Strike Debt Assembly 2012, p. 2)

This way of "tying together" diverse struggles is fundamental: the dimension of financial disobedience is also a struggle for public services, for recognition of labor that has historically been devalued and not remunerated by wages (Federici 2016). That same type of diagram is what is drawn by the feminist strike.

WE WANT OURSELVES ALIVE AND DEBT FREE!

Through the action on June 2, 2017, led by the Ni Una Menos Collective, when we shouted "We Want Ourselves Alive and Debt Free" in front of the Central Bank of the Argentine Republic, where we passed out fliers and read a manifesto with that same title, we brought private, household, and family debt onto the public stage and into debate as a feminist issue.

We asked ourselves what it means to be insubordinate to finance (that was the name of the broader collective that organized the action). In that way, we started to problematize the abstract dynamic of finance in relation to everyday life, to the forms of violence in households and diverse territories, and to current modes of labor exploitation.

That action had multiple resonances. One of the most interesting ones was that for the Ni Una Menos March on June 4, 2018, different unions appropriated that slogan for their calls. In the lead up to this march, one of the most accelerated processes of public indebtedness in Argentinean history was getting underway, which ended with negotiations with the IMF, a brutal devaluation of wages, and cuts to the public budget that included the elimination of 13 ministries.

US AGAINST DEBT

In 2019, the images of "combative *perreo*" from Puerto Rico traveled the world showing the rhythm of protest, waving bodies and flags as a reaction to the misogynist, homophobic, and racist chats of its governor, Ricardo Rossello, who has since resigned. What one sees in those viral photos and videos, however, is not merely a bit of added color or spontaneity. We are seeing mobilizations with a feminist, queer, and popular composition in a colonial territory of the United States. There, people have been weaving together self-management and resistance in the face of the economic crisis, especially following the effects of the tragedy of Hurricane Maria in 2017 (the topic of another one of the official's chats, uncovered by a group of journalists). One of the organizations targeted by those official insults was, not coincidentally, key in the organizational fabric of the mobilizations, the Colectiva Feminista en Construcción (Feminist Collective in Construction).

That collective vindicates a way of using the body that produces the density of the mobilizations, the texture of the protest, and a way of posing the conflict: the violence of a colonial state that creates debt and makes life precarious can only be confronted by dismantling the intersecting hierarchies of race, gender, and class. The Colectiva Feminista en Construcción also put forth the slogan "March 8: Us against the debt" in 2019, in the heat of the international feminist strikes, in a country with a record level of femicides, as well as a record level of debt.

It is important to remember Puerto Rico's political status: it is an unincorporated territory of the United States, which means that Puerto Rico belongs to the United States, but is not part of it. A year before the hurricane, in 2016, a "Fiscal Control Board" dedicated to restructuring the territory's debt landed on the island: a new form of colonial government that, on the one hand, exempts the United States from taking responsibility for its annexed territories and, on the other, ensures that the debt is paid. In other words, debt restructuring is the only option and, to do so, an elite is directly established to design the restructuring and supervise the local government. Puerto Rico is an extreme example but demonstrates the modus operandi of "foreign" debt in Latin America as a mechanism of discipline and recolonization.

Colectiva Feminista en Construcción, however, has been in the streets well before those chats were made public and those messages express much more than an outburst: they clarify how debt and its colonial political forms are based on the exploitation of and simultaneous disregard for the lives and desires of autonomy of Black women, the poor, and the LGBTQI community.

On November 25, 2018, they carried out a protest in front of the government house, known as La Fortaleza, claiming that while the government's main concern was to keep bondholders happy, no action was being taken against the increase in gender-based violence. A few days earlier they called a "Plantón against Machista Violence." For the feminist strike on March 8, 2018 they held a protest called "Feminist Embargo" in the Plaza Las Américas shopping mall, in which they highlighted the bank's role in the housing and debt crisis facing the country. They denounced the banks Santander, Banco Popular, Oriental Bank, and First Bank, rendering visible their responsibility for the number of foreclosures and people left homeless. They emphasized that only one year before hurricanes Irma and Maria left millions without a home, the banks also played their part, dispossessing 5554 families.

As Rocío Zambrana (2019) argues, discussing Puerto Rico's debt, it is necessary to foreground these debts as "colonial debts." She points out how that mechanism originated in Haiti: "The only successful slave revolution in history was neutralized through debt. Today, the population of Haiti lives in poverty, subject to the interests of capital managed by states and international institutions such as the IMF." For Puerto Rico, the possibility of subverting debt, as Zambrana argues, citing Ariadna Godreau-Aubert's (2018) work, traces and seeks to revert the relationship between debt, austerity, and coloniality. Godreau-Aubert says that it is necessary to reveal the "pedagogy of indebted women" whose indebted life is what effectively produces the continuation of the colonial condition.

Thus, plurinational, anticolonial, and popular feminisms are particularly capable of responding to the systematic indebtedness of our countries and household economies. They manage to concretely demonstrate the effects of debt on everyday life. And they do so through mobilization and street action: from public denunciations of banking institutions to the detailed analysis of who is affected by the dispossession of land and public services, the increase in housing rents, and the modes of managing precarization. But debt is also inseparable from the disciplining of bodies, habits, and desires against which the combative *perreo* and the debt audit form a common program.

"THEY OWE US A LIFE"

We are witnessing the increasingly brutal and violent deployment of a patriarchal, racist, and colonial geopolitics. The strikes and mobilizations that started in October 2019 in Ecuador and continued in Chile and Colombia synthesize the scene of dispossession at the hands of global finance that led to an uprising across the territory.

Let's turn to what happened in Chile: we see the slogans and practices of the feminist strike acting at the mass level as a plurinational general strike. It is an accumulation of experiences that has managed to change the texture of struggles, their organizational forms, their political formulas, their historical alliances. We see it expressed on the walls. We'll take two examples: "They owe us a life," as a synthesis that reverses the debt, who owes whom, graffitied on banks in the country of the Chicago Boys, with the highest level of per capita debt in the region. Faced with the increase in the cost of everyday life, that is, the extraction of value from each moment of social reproduction, they propose financial disobedience with the slogan-practice "Massive Evasion." The second example of graffiti-synthesis is "Fascist, Pig, your daughter is a feminist" (*Paco, fascista, tu hija es feminista*), which points to the profound destablization of patriarchy to which the fascism of our times is responding, to both its structural and micropolitical filigree. Student debt and the privatization of pensions in private investment funds in particular, and more broadly, debt as a mode of life, were some of the key issues in the general feminist strike against the precarization of life that took place in Chile in 2020.

The battle lines are clearly drawn: the plurinationality of struggles against the globality of finance. The transnational dynamic of struggles has rendered visible how neo-extractivism functions as a formula for recolonizing the continent and it has put the new forms of exploitation of historically disregarded and badly paid work up for debate. Therefore, it is not a coincidence that plurinationality, driven by Indigenous struggles, today comes forward as a banner of encounters, assemblies, and protests. Plurinationality is the expression of a concrete composition of the most vital struggles against the neoliberal and conservative alliances. In Argentina, it is led by Indigenous women who sought to plurinationalize the Encuentro Nacional de Mujeres (National Women's Gathering)[5] with the slogan #NosQueremosPlurinacional (#WeWantToBePlurinational), campaigns led by many different organizations and collectives who

---

5.   The Encuentro Nacional de Mujeres has been held annually, rotating between different cities in Argentina, since 1986 and regularly draws tens of thousands of participants for self-organized workshops. In recent years, there has been a strong push by Indigenous movements for recognition and inclusion, calling for a Plurinational Encounter of Women, Lesbians, Travestis, Trans, and Non-binary People.

shout #SomosPlurinacional (#WeArePlurinational), the compañeras of the #MigrarNoEsDelito (Migrating is not a crime) campaign, of NiUnaMigranteMenos, and the historical plurinational composition of feminist assemblies and social movements. That plurinationality is also that of the Indigenous protagonism pushed the #ElParoNoPara (#TheStrikeDoesn'tStop) and the resistance of women against the paquetazo of neoliberal reforms in Ecuador in 2019, artifices of the recent Plurinational Women's Parliament and feminist organizations.

It is an accumulation of struggles that has the concrete task of decolonizing our language and practices, our imaginaries and our bodies. And, above all, of expanding that plurinational dynamic to other debates: for example, the union debate. Compañeras from the Comité de Trabajadores y Sindicalistas de la Coordinadora 8M de Chile (Committee of Workers and Unionists of Chile's 8M Coordinator) are thinking about a "plurinational system of care." The plurinational, as a concrete transnational force, is also a perspective and a method that allows for weaving a common agenda that includes the body-territories that nourish the feminisms mobilizing across Abya Yala.

A FEMINIST STRIKE AGAINST DEBT: 2020

We have shown how the transnational feminist movement has taken up the struggle against debt as a banner of struggle as part of the dynamics of the feminist strike. Around the world we have said, "We want ourselves alive and debt free!" (Argentina), "It is us against debt!" (Puerto Rico), "They owe us a Life!" (Chile), "We don't owe, we won't pay!" (Spain). It is historic: the feminist movement is politicizing, at the mass scale, the financial issue. And, it is a feminist analysis of debt that allows us to rethink economic violence in terms of its relation with sexist violence. The feminist strike, by denouncing the debt with the IMF and private creditors and its impact on household debts, continues to make other debts appear, rendering them visible and reclaiming them. While bondholders and investment funds apply pressure to collect on all of their investments, on the streets it becomes clear that we are the creditors.

This has not been accomplished haphazardly. A fundamental inversion has taken place, demonstrated in workplaces and in homes, in front of banks and against transnational corporations, showing that we do not owe anything. We know that debt is a historical mechanism of capitalism used to loot, exploit, and privatize the commons that we create and re-create, as well as to increase labor exploitation in moments of crisis. The most well known of these mechanisms is the way in which public debt conditions states. This is a constant, cyclical scene in Latin America, but also more broadly as a global colonial circuit.

It is only more recently, however, that the circuits connecting that public debt with their effects in everyday life have been traced. This has been accomplished because women, lesbians, travestis, trans, and non-binary people resist and put words to the experience of simultaneously being over-exploited as workers in the labor market and as domestic workers, as consumers, and now also as debtors.

Connecting debt, violence, and labor has also been achieved by the feminist strikes. In the call for the fourth international strike, in Argentina, the discussion of debt was woven together in different territories with a productive and reproductive strike in a two-day event: March 8th and 9th. It was also expressed with the main slogan: "The debt is owed to us, not the IMF or the churches," demonstrating both a precise diagnosis of the conjuncture and of the movement's broader horizon. Saying "we want to be debt free" in slums and in unions, on the streets and in the university is a method of analysis and action that connects finance to bodies.

But debating debt does not only mean talking about debt. Debt is directly connected with budget cuts to public services, wage decreases, with the recognition of domestic work, and with the need to go into debt to get an abortion. We only go into debt because we have already been left without other resources. Debt only comes to "save us" because we have been violently impoverished, to the point of an induced precarity. Debt becomes unpayable because first there was looting and dispossession.

Speaking of debt from a feminist perspective allows us to clearly see what is feeding the global flows of financial capital, which seek to appropriate pensions, wages, and an enormous quantity of free and precarious labor that is what moves the world today, that drives extractivist dispossession and enables the extraordinary profitability of multinational corporations. We have identified and denounced this operation due to its direct connection with the increase in labor, institutional, racist, and sexist forms of violence.

Let's look at a practical example of a financial geography that is rendered visible by the feminist strike. The investment fund BlackRock, which is one of the largest holders of Argentine debt under foreign legislation, is the same fund that has enormous investments in Mexican pension funds and that is demanding an adjustment to the retirement system there. We must shine light on the connection between financial speculation, an increase to the retirement age, and the non-recognition of the labor of women, lesbians, travestis, and trans people: the profits of the investment fund are guaranteed by extending the years of over-exploitation of that labor. But, additionally, the assets of these investment funds (the money they capture from retirees who pay more for longer) allow them to buy up and privatize public companies. With one move, those workers are forced to work longer and dispossessed of public services, and thus their income is also devalued (as they now have to pay for services that used to be public and free).

This dynamic of dispossession, which accumulates through violence against certain bodies and territories, can help explain why the feminist strike took off more forcefully in Mexico in 2020 in comparison with earlier years. According to official agencies, the country averages ten femicides per day. The call for the strike on March 8 and 9 went viral with different slogans, such as "A day without women" and "Nobody moves on the 9th," that express an organizational accumulation of an "unfurling of rage" as several activists explain. The Zapatistas, university students, artists, and feminist collectives from across the country joined the call, as well as women workers in the maquilas, struggling against some of the harshest employers on the continent.

Undoubtedly, what is woven together with increasing force is the link between gender-based violence and political and economic violence. That same investment fund that lands in Argentina and Mexico, aspiring to social wealth, is denounced by the Yellow Vests in France: they accuse it of being complicit in the pension reforms driven by president Emmanuel Macron that were recently the impetus for mass protests. The strike that lasted more than 40 days in that country – including everyone from the national opera's ballet dancers to the railway workers – was another powerful scene of the effects of financial expropriation of wages and pensions.

Therefore, the mode of operation of investment funds (which are fundamental actors in the renegotiation of the national debt) cannot be explained through methodological nationalism: they are fueled by the pension funds of one country that they use to buy public debt from another country with financing needs, that in turn they can invest in other places by buying mortgage debts or investing in energy. This has also been shown by the Platform of People Affected by Mortgages (PAH), which has protested against evictions across Spain due to financial bubbles. In 2018, the PAH filed a lawsuit against BlackRock for its role in causing inflation in housing prices.

Since then, this denunciation has been a central part of feminist and migrant mobilizations and, in particular, it has enabled a connection to be made between the March 8 feminist strike and actions against evictions and for the right to housing. The unionization of renters shakes up the "stop evictions" campaign, putting names and faces to the struggle (#GiselliSeQueda #GiselliIsNotGoingAnywhere) and defending renters from house to house. "Since its beginning, feminist practice has been central to the PAH, because its activism was always made up of housewives, elderly women, and migrant women, especially from South America. The crisis of traditional couples is also connected to defaults on housing payments and it is usually women who stay in the house with debt," says Lotta Merri Priti Tenhuhen, a PAH activist in the Vallekas neighborhood of Madrid. For the 2020 March 8 strike, a PAH communique stated:

> We are the ones who confront the real estate scam. We refuse to pay abusive rents. We refuse to stay on the street. The struggle for housing is a feminist struggle. Many of us have experienced sexist violence in our own homes, as well as on the streets and at work. We invite other feminist comrades to join the movement for housing, side by side, to stop evictions, reclaim houses, fight against the banks and vulture funds, to demand rights and carry them out in practice through mutual aid, and to struggle so that life be in the center.

In this feminist strike, we can trace the geography of dispossession and expropriation that are taken advantage of by so-called "investment windfalls." Struggles for housing, waged recognition, pensions, they are all part of the same program of financial disobedience.

As we discussed above, in Argentina, retirement benefits have also been a key issue in recent feminist mobilizations. The complicity between union and feminist actions and languages has been fundamental. Under the slogan "All Women are Workers," the alliance has been able to problematize labor in its multiplicity of forms. Experimentation with practices of social unionism that bring together issues of rent and labor, pensions and popular economy, the denunciation of sexual abuse and labor violence, would be impossible without feminism. It is not a coincidence that murals stating "It's not love, its unpaid labor" have been painted in several union headquarters. By inverting the hierarchy of recognition of unpaid labor, it also inverts the burden of debt. The debt belongs to the state, the bosses, and the patriarchs for having benefited from this historically free and compulsory labor.

The forms of evasion, of denunciation of the feminization of poverty and generalized dispossessions, of the precarity of labor and every life, weave together questions. By asking how to carry out a strike against finance, we also ask what our debts are made of and who claims to have the right to control our existences.

Femicides and travesticides are inseparable from this geography of capital that imposes increasingly violent forms of dispossession and exploitation around the world. Saying "the debt is owed to us" in the international feminist strike *inverts* the burden of the debt: it recognizes us as the creditors and it forces investigations about debt to start in households and on the streets.

Excursus

Rosa Luxemburg: In the Lands of Debt and Consumption

Here we have been trying to analyze debt as a generalized mechanism of dispossession. David Harvey's (2003) formula of "accumulation by dispossession" has been widely used in recent years to discuss capitalism's contemporary form. According to Harvey, today capital recreates the methods of the moment of so-called "primitive accumulation" to compulsively expropriate new resources for its valorization, displacing the mode of exploitation of labor power under the Fordist model. One of Harvey's fundamental references is Rosa Luxemburg's reflection on the expansive dynamic of capital to account for a "new" imperialism. Emphasizing the necessity of multiple "outsides" to enable that growing push of the frontiers of valorization, it is Luxemburg who can provide key elements for understanding the current forms of dispossession, of extractivism, particularly if we expand the extractive question to finance, under the interpretative key of *financial extractivism*.

Financialization (also addressed by Lenin in terms of imperialism) expresses the extension of the logic of capital accumulation in which its inherent contradiction is knotted together. In Luxemburg's terms, it is about the spatial and temporal gap between the production of surplus value and its conversion into capital in the first place. But that implies a *prior* question: the relationship between capital and its "outsides."

In *The Accumulation of Capital* (1913), explaining the ideal theoretical schema in which Marx addresses production and the realization of surplus value between figures of "capitalists" and "workers," Luxemburg proposes expanding the figures in a non-formal way, opening a way for the pluralization that seems to be revealed as inherent to consumption. "The decisive fact is that the surplus value cannot be realized by sale either to workers or to capitalists, but only if it is sold to such social organizations or strata whose own mode of production is not capitalistic" (p. 317). She gives the example of the English cotton textile industry that for two-thirds of the nineteenth century supplied India, America, and

Africa, while also providing to peasants and the European petite bour-geoisie. She concludes: "*The enormous expansion of the English cotton industry was thus founded on consumption by non-capitalist strata and countries*" (italics in the original).

The *very elasticity of the accumulation process* involves the immanent contradiction indicated previously. Capital's "revolutionary" effect operates in those displacements, capable of quickly resolving the discon-tinuity of the social process of accumulation. To that "magical art" of capital, Luxemburg adds the necessity of the non-capitalist: "but only on the pre-capitalist soil of more primitive social conditions can it develop the ascendancy necessary to achieve such miracles" (p. 324).

The violence of that appropriation by European capital requires a complementary political power that is only identified with non-Euro-pean conditions: that is, the power exercised in American, Asian, and African "colonies." Here Luxemburg cites the exploitation of Indige-nous peoples by the Peruvian Amazon Co. Ltd. that supplied London with Amazon rubber to demonstrate how capital manages to produce a situation "bordering on slavery." "International trade" as a "prime necessity for the historical existence of capitalism" then appears as "an exchange between capitalistic and non-capitalistic modes of production" (p. 325). But what emerges when the accumulation process is considered from the point of view of variable capital, that is, of living labor (and not only of surplus and fixed capital)?

The "natural" and "social" limits to the increase in exploitation of the labor force mean that accumulation, Luxemburg says, should increase the number of employed workers. Marx's quote about how capitalist pro-duction has been concerned with "establishing the working class as a class dependent on the wage" leads to the question of the "natural pro-creation of the working class" that, however, does not follow the rhythms and movements of capital. But, Luxemburg argues, "Labor for this army is recruited from social reservoirs outside the dominion of capital – it is drawn into the wage proletariat only if need arises. Only the existence of non-capitalist groups and countries can guarantee such a supply of addi-tional labor power for capitalist production" (p. 327).

Luxemburg adds the question of race: as capital needs to have access to "all territories and climes," "nor can it function solely with the workers offered by the white race": "It must be able to mobilize world labor power without restriction in order to utilize all productive forces of the globe – up to the limits imposed by a system of producing surplus value" (p.

328). The point is that those workers of the non-white race "must first be 'set free' in order to be enrolled in the active army of capital." Recruitment, from this point of view, follows the *liberating* orientation that is attributed to the proletariat understood as a "free" subject (Luxemburg cites the South African diamond mines as an example).

The "labor problem in the colonies" is thus a mixture of work situations ranging from the wage to other less "pure" modes of contraction. But we are interested in how Luxemburg highlights the "contemporary existence" of non-capitalist elements in capitalism as a key element for its expansion. This is the starting point for re-evaluating the problem of the internal and external market, which she emphasizes are not only concepts of political geography, but primarily of social economy. The conversion of surplus value into capital, seen in this map of global dependency, is revealed at the same time as "ever more urgent and precarious" (p. 333).

But let's go a step farther. Capital can by force, Luxemburg says, appropriate the means of production and also force workers to become an object of capitalist exploitation. What it cannot do by violence is "force them to buy its commodities": that is, it cannot force them to "realize its surplus value" (p. 353). In other words, it cannot force them to become consumers.

Here we can extend her reasoning to current conditions, adding an element: the way of becoming consumers in large sectors of the planet is through mass indebtedness. A particular form of producing the "obligation" necessary so that commodities are realized. This introduces a fundamental *financial* violence in the realization of commodities. But the novelty of our present moment is that contemporary indebtedness does not need waged workers in order to be successful.

There is a fundamental articulation between international credit, infrastructure, and commodity placement. Luxemburg analyzes this in detail in several passages: in the struggle against all the "formations of the natural economy" and particularly in the dispossession of lands to put an end to the self-sufficiency of peasant economies, highlighting the mortgage debts of American farmers and Dutch and English imperialist policy in South Africa against Black and Indigenous populations as concrete forms of political violence, tax pressure, and the introduction of cheap goods.

Debt is that apparatus that puts the focus on the problem of the temporal and spatial gap between the realization and capitalization of surplus value; and thus the necessity of *colonial* expansion. Luxemburg dedicates several emblematic paragraphs on this operation of debt to the relationship between England and the Argentine Republic, where lending, the English exportation of manufactured goods, and the construction of railways reached astronomical figures in merely a decade and a half. South American states, South African colonies, and other "exotic countries" (Turkey and Greece for example) equally attracted capital flows in cycles punctuated by bankruptcies and later restarted: "Realized surplus value, that in England or Germany cannot be capitalized and remains inactive, is inverted in Argentina, Australia, the Cape or Mesopotamia in railways, hydraulic works, mines, etc." (p. 394). The (temporal and spatial) dislocation referring to where and when surplus value can be capitalized allows accumulation to function like a machine of abstraction that, however, depends on the concrete circumstances that it attempts to homogenize time and time again: "English capital that flowed into Argentina for the construction of railroads can be Indian opium introduced to China" (p. 395).

Abroad, however, a "new demand" must be made to emerge or "violently created": what is moved, Luxemburg says, is the "enjoyment" of the products. But how are the conditions produced so that this *enjoyment* takes place? "It is certain that the 'enjoyment' of the products must be realized, must be paid for by the new consumers. Therefore, the new consumers must have money" (p. 394). Today, the massification of indebtedness crowns the production of that enjoyment. This enjoyment is the translation of a desire that produces an *outside*. Of course it is not a strictly literal or territorial outside.

What pre-announces the crisis in Luxemburg's argument is the catastrophic moment of the end of the non-capitalist world to be appropriated through imperialist expansion. In the current permanent displacement of those limits (and constant management of the crisis), there is something we should see under the surface: the creation of non-capitalist worlds (space-times of desire), which capital rushes to with increasing voracity, velocity, and intensity. At the same time, we must also detect what type of extractive operations relaunch the *imperial* question, now going beyond national limits.

Luxemburg's clues shine today for our project of constructing a political critique of the economy based on feminist movements and perspectives.

Some Milestones of a Brief Chronology

In November 2016, the Central Bank of the Republic of Argentina (BCRA) authorized the creation of savings accounts and debit cards for minors to "facilitate their everyday economic operations, stimulate financial education for youth, and promote bankarization through the use of electronic payment methods."

In March 2017, the Ciudad Microempresas firm, made up of Banco Ciudad de Buenos Aires (Bank of the City of Buenos Aires) and Corporación Buenos Aires Sur bought Cordial Microfinanzas from Banco Supervielle for $46.5 million. The firm has a loan portfolio of $192 million and operates out of five branches: the neighborhood of Flores, Villa Celina, Laferre, Olmos (all low-income neighborhoods or towns in the city of Buenos Aires or its suburbs), and La Salada market (the largest informal market on the continent).

In July 2017, the National Executive, through a necessity and urgency decree, implemented a line of personal credit for retirees and pensioners and beneficiaries of the Universal Child Allowance subsidy, with interest rates of around 24 percent annually.

In October 2018, one of the most important themes of the meeting of the W20, the G20's women's "affinity group," was the promotion of financial inclusion of poor women, based on the diagnosis that a "financial gap" – that is, the difference between the number of men and women included in the financial system – is one of the reasons for the higher poverty rate among women. Queen Máxima of the Netherlands also participated in the exhibition as a UN representative on issues of inclusive financing for development and as the honorary president of the G20's Global Alliance for Financial Inclusion "promoting the expansion of microcredit for women as a privileged form of fighting poverty."

On November 28, 2018, the Central Bank (BCRA) approved resolution number A6603 that incorporates a new complementary service to financial activity called "banking correspondents," which means that those entities can delegate customer attention to businesses, gas stations, supermarkets, pharmacies, or physical persons using the human resources of the correspondents in accordance with an agreement with the banks that allows them to carry out all sorts of banking operations.

On December 26, 2018, the Central Bank (BCRA), through communication "A" 6619, relieved currency exchange agencies from the obligation to present Reports of Suspicious Operations. That measure represents a virtual free pass for money laundering in the exchange market.

Argentina's foreign debt increased by $56,665 million over the course of one year and reached $261,483 million in the second trimester of 2018 (according to the National Institute of Statistics and Census, INDEC). The availability of data on public debt lies in sharp contrast to the difficulty in finding statistics on private debt.

Interviews

The interviews compiled here with compañeras from different types of activist organizations narrate concrete tactics of fighting debt, everyday forms of its refusal. On the one hand, they discuss alternative forms of loans and financing that emerge from social organizations. These are able to help people's economic projects without high interest rates and without extortionary persecution when people have difficulties making payment deadlines. For now, as the interviewees comment, this financial infrastructure does not have the size and scale that would allow it to replace other credit providers, but it is an initiative that they are trying to strengthen.

On the other hand, migrants from Bolivia living in Argentina return to using the community savings institution, the *pasanaku* (which has been fundamental for the self-construction of *villas* and popular commercial networks) as a form of debt relief. This way, they collect money to "save" the indebted women, who take turns receiving the funds, based on an institution that combines a game and trust.

From the experiences of women denied freedom or in situations of transition or recently liberated, collective organization appears as the first tool to confront that system of complex debt that links and traces a continuum from inside to outside of the prison. In that same register, women from Manaus start talking about the "scam" among themselves, putting everyday difficulties in common and "occupying" the institution that places them in debt. Thus, narrating and occupying, they "unravel" the opaque and hidden circuit of debt.

"Debt affects your health, and you stop doing things in your free time to be able to generate more money"

*A large assembly of women, lesbians, travestis, and trans people meets weekly in the neighborhood of Lugano. They are members of the **Federación de Organizaciones de Base** (FOB, or Federation of Grassroots Organizations), which is also part of the National Campaign against Violence against Women. The FOB is a social movement with an anarchist tendency* *that was formed in 2006. It brings together neighborhood political organizations from across the country. It is part of the piquetero, or unemployed workers' movement, and is defined by principles of direct democracy, self-management, class independence, federalism, and feminism. The majority of this assembly's members are migrants and workers in cooperatives who do neighborhood cleaning or work in the organization's print shop. We spoke to a few women in an assembly who told us how they are forced to take out debt because of inflation and austerity measures, and how that then forces them to accept jobs under ever worse conditions. But they also spoke of alternative forces of financing that help them to get out of debt. This conversation took place while preparing for the assembly to plan for November 26, a transnational day of action against violence against women, lesbians, trans people, and travestis. Debt was discussed as a form of economic violence and as part of the web of violence against which we organize ourselves.*

We are part of a cooperative, we work cleaning the street. I also clean in a private home. However since everything is so expensive now, it is not enough for us. We used to work less and I could get by.

Have you taken out any type of debt?
Not for now, I don't want to because it is a big commitment. Now we are dealing with the issue of our house because our neighborhood is undergoing redevelopment and we don't know if we will have to leave or if we will be able to stay and all of that. And with more debt, where could I get the money to pay for everything?

You see that in Ribeiro [household appliance store] when you take out debt and you don't pay it back or if you are behind on a payment, they charge you tremendous interest. My uncle bought a television in Ribeiro, and that television, he paid double or triple, it was like buying three TVs.

Because he fell behind on the payments?
Yes and then the interest rate was very high.

Here I work in the cooperative and I am part of the printing press. I still don't work anywhere else. I used to work more but I stopped because the truth is that now there isn't even work anywhere else, and besides threads are expensive. I worked in textiles and I also took out credit from Coppel [department store].

Coppel?
Yes, Coppel, I got some shoes that cost 1500 pesos and I fell behind with the payment and the debt multiplied, as if I were buying three pairs of shoes, that is, it tripled. That's why now I don't take out any more loans anywhere, not in Ribeiro or in Coppel. Because I have the cards. They offered me credit but I don't do it because the truth is my life is very difficult now. There is a lot of poverty, the money from work is not enough. And also the Institute of Cooperative Housing is coming to my house, and I don't know if I'll get assistance, I don't think I am going to get it. So I stopped a bit. Anyway, now they offered me a loan to build my house.

Who offered it to you?
I don't know if they are from the housing office or what, but they offered it to me, and I told them no because I'm not in much of a hurry to build my house. I am going to do it calmly. I don't want to be pressured to feel, "I owe money, I have to pay" and that's why I didn't take out a loan.

The money that you don't have, that you need in order to live, how are you getting it?
I don't know, I am supporting myself somehow. I don't have children either. There is a lot of hunger and there are older women who are not united in any organization and now it is also very difficult to obtain a DNI [National Identification Document], which you need, because you have to pay 10,000 pesos. And then the truth is that they can't join an organization because they don't have a DNI and, yes they can participate to receive food, but they can't join like we have.

And do you have any friends who are in debt?
Yes, in fact I have a compañera who got into debt like that and she had to pay.

She bought, I think, a stereo system and she couldn't pay for it and she had to hand over all of her *pasanaku* to pay off her debt. The *pasanaku* is a type of savings between compañeras, like a loan but without interest.

You need something and you get a number, that is, the money that we have rotates between us.

Pasanaku is a word that in Quechua means "pass the hand," meaning you have to pass it around. Something that you get and you give in return. It is a game where you gather, let's say ten people, those ten people get together and each month, depending on how you go about organizing it, it can be monthly, weekly, or biweekly. And you get together with those people and say, well "how much?" I put in 100 pesos, she puts in 100, another woman puts in 100. Here we raised 500 and we say each week we have to raise 500, we have to put in 100 each week. Then there is a lottery. It is a secret lottery, each woman takes out one number. You could end up with 1, 2, 3, 4, 5. The first week that we gather the 500, we give it to you. The second week it is her turn to take the 500; that is, you come with your 100 again, she comes with her 100, and so on.

Are all the women part of this?
Yes, since we are all compañeras.

We have organized among ourselves to play this way, each time that we get our monthly payment for working in the cooperative, we put a small part in the *pasanaku*.

Today, what is the pasanaku mostly used for?
To get out of debt, like my friend did, right?

A compañera was in debt and she used it all to pay it off?
Yes, to pay it off, so that they didn't keep raising her interest payments.

And it works for you like that, if I draw number 5, when you all give me the $500, I can make a big purchase of something, an important product or something.

And you don't go into debt, right?
Right, everyone receives the same amount and there is no interest or anything, because this way of doing things has been used for many years; in fact that that is why we use the word *pasanaku*, it comes from Quechua. It has been used for years and years, I remember that my mom

always played. Once my mom had gone into a ton of debt, she had put up the papers on my house and all of that.

Where had she gotten it?
There in Bolivia, in the Banco Unión.

What was it for?
It was to be able to start building a shack to live in. My mom had seven children and so we needed more space and she went into debt for that. And ever since that moment I have hated debt. I never bought anything like that in installments. Because they tell you that there is no interest and this and that, but when you finish paying and calculate how much you paid, the amount is much higher and there is interest involved.

Debt limits you in different ways because it affects your health, and you stop doing things in your free time to be able to generate more money. I know several people who have to constantly pay a certain amount of money each month and then the stress begins, the headaches, "where I am going to get money," or "I'll take out a loan from somewhere else to be able to pay and then I have to pay that," and it starts eating up next month too. Thus, like always, it creates a never-ending chain. It is very complicated to live like that and it affects you in every way, because it also puts you in a bad mood, there is a lot of pressure. You put aside your children because you have to go out and earn money, that happens a lot.

And what type of jobs does someone get when they are in debt?
Under the table jobs, and on top of that, they pay you less, but it is better to earn a little than nothing at all. I have seen a lot of people like that.

When a person owes money to someone, sometimes the woman who loaned it is in need and then, what can she do? They clash, they argue, they fight. "You have to get it for me right now! Because I need it!" and sometimes the woman doesn't have it. And where is she going to go? She has to go to someone else and perhaps she can't obtain it and then she goes around feeling really bad, and sometimes her blood pressure rises, sometimes she is worried and doesn't sleep. I also went through this with my mom. My mom, to put food on the table for us, had to borrow from a woman and sometimes it wasn't enough and then she had to borrow from someone else and it wouldn't be enough and it kept going like that.

That happened here?
No, that was in Bolivia, since we didn't have a house, my mom paid rent, and sometimes she didn't pay it and the woman kicked us out. That's why I'm very sensitive toward people who are having a hard time here.

Where are the places where the financial companies offer credit?
In the neighborhood. They go to the school exit, for example.

They also go to the clinic where you take your children to the doctor or to the market where people are constantly circulating. It is like the neighborhood's main street. And they go there and say, "you only need your ID card," "you only need your ID card."

I have seen Ribeiro and Coppel a lot recently, I have also seen Cencosud [retail company] a lot. Within the *villa* [slum], it is terrible.

Do they offer more to women or to men?
To us women.

And why to you all, do you think?
Because we are responsible for our homes and we are the ones who see what is needed in our households and that is why they come and offer more to women and they say "if you affiliate now, we will give you the card and you can go ahead and take out a certain amount." They talk to you about amounts with which you can start to buy, "if you go ahead and take out the card now, next week you can withdraw what you want from the agency and you have an amount of 3000 or 4000 pesos to be able to spend and you'll go about paying it off."

They even give you pamphlets saying that as an affiliate you have a 20%, a 10% discount.

They sweet talk you more than anything, because it is not so much that you say "Oh, look I already have this and I am going to take some out." Then the month ends and it's not enough and then the problem comes, like she was saying, we get stressed, we have high blood pressure, because there is never enough money and this also affects our health a lot, as well as our families and everything. Because sometimes when a mother feels bad, then the whole house is no longer well, because the ones running the households are usually women.

Well one woman took out loans like that with a card and she went to pick up the products and then she couldn't pay, and later her husband told her "you're the one getting involved in those things, you bought things and now you can't pay. Now deal with it."

What did she buy?
A blender and a refrigerator.

That is why we help each other among women. For the *pasanaku* we all meet up in someone's house and when the numbers are ready and all rolled up in a bag, then they come and see how many of us there are, say there are ten of us, then here are ten numbers. Then we place the ten numbers in the bag and everyone grabs one, they are sorted and you note them down. You see who drew 1, who drew 2, and so on, and you write everything down and every month you have to organize it so that everyone comes and brings the money to be able to collect it. And it is all collected.

And that is between women?
Some men also get involved.

And if there is a compañera who is very bad off economically, can some sort of exception be made?
If there is an emergency, the number can be exchanged for a closer one.

When it is her turn and she gives me the money that was going to be hers. And it's always the same, because we already trust one another.

Because you have to be very committed. Especially if it lands on you the first round, you have to keep paying every month.

That is why we do it between compañeras, I never had any problems.

"With debt, we are involuntary subjected to financing the patriarchy's time"

Eva Reinoso is a member of the feminist collective YoNoFui, which works in between the inside and outside of the prison walls. YoNoFui emerged out of a poetry workshop in the Penitentiary Unit No. 31 of Ezeiza, in the province of Buenos Aires. The collective works with women and trans people who are currently incarcerated or under house arrest, or who have passed through the prison system. Its work focuses on creating spaces for artistic expression and skills training. Some time ago we read a poem that Eva wrote, "We want to be debt free!" Based on that text, we spoke with her about debt as a constant link between inside and outside of the prison, debt for abortions and debt for consumption. We also talked about jobs that "are invented" to generate an income and, finally, why debt funds the patriarchy's time.

Let's see if I understood correctly: there are certain jobs available in federal prisons but not for everyone.
There are jobs for part of the population, 70% of the population, but for the rest there is nothing, it comes and goes, it comes and goes. But there is work that is guaranteed and remunerated for 70% of the population. But not in the Buenos Aires prisons.

In the Buenos Aires ones you work, but they don't pay you?
In the Buenos Aires prisons you work, but they pay you 16 cents an hour. In other words, there are young women sentenced to five years, working, doing cleaning or cooking or what have you, and they get out and for those five years of work they give them 250 bucks! They do slave labor for the good behavior, in reality. Because if you refuse to do that, when they have to make a report about you in court, it goes badly, they don't do it or they do it badly. But well, women, even with all of that, take whatever they are given and engineer it and create strategies for generating resources on the outside, because they can make you a stuffed animal using a curtain and with a box of cigarettes they make an ashtray, and they exchange it for a phone card or they sell it to someone to give a birthday present to their partner, and thus they go about gathering a bit of money. In the textile workshop in José León Suárez prison, where I teach with two other compañeras, the young women make everything from underwear, dolls, ashtrays, anything you could imagine. Everything with nothing because sometimes we take scraps that people give us and we take things and later the following Friday you and they have produced

something incredible, from things that leave you asking: how do they do it? And they sell them and make money to have on the outside.

What is it like to be in debt in prison, especially in terms of that relationship with the outside that you were talking about before?
Yes, when you are inside prison you are in debt, because you have to pay for a lawyer and you sell your house so that they'll let you out, when you have a kid on the outside and you have to keep paying electricity, gas, you have to keep paying everything, because the majority are single mothers and heads of households.

They keep working inside the prison to pay their bills outside?
Yes, because most of them don't have a single peso to buy soap, or rather they prefer to buy food from the cart and not buy themselves anything, except for buying something to share during the visits. That is why I say that women from inside prison are sustaining their families on the outside with all the limitations that they have, they keep doing it with the income that they obtain through work and in the Buenos Aires prisons without any type of income, nothing. They do magic, to put it one way, because they literally take a rag and make a doll out of it, they sell it to you and obtain some cash so that their family can get there to visit or to pay, I don't know, the phone bill, or what have you. In comparison to the men, that is something that doesn't happen with them, because in the men's prisons you see the lines and lines of women carrying bundles of things to support the men. The guys, on the other hand, blow it, they spend it on themselves, and you go to the women's prison and there are always women: relatives, mothers, sisters, aunts. You never see a line of guys waiting to enter with packages for the women.

Right, it is always other women who take them things.
Yes, and that is what I was saying in the text that we made based on Ni Una Menos's text about debt. We have to decide what debt we leave for the coming month, because you can't cover everything. For example, this month, you see how the electricity bill comes bimonthly? I have to see if I'll pay the gas or if I pay the electricity and go about alternating like that. One month I'll pay the electricity, one month the gas, one month water, and so on, like a circuit that I go about prioritizing, according to what they are closest to cutting off. I got out of prison in 2012 and it was like that.

And when you were in prison, were you in debt?
No, I didn't have children, therefore I wasn't in debt with the outside. But I got into debt on the inside with those who sold for substance abuse, for example. There is also a whole sector that works to pay for their drugs. And that is also totally approved by the service. It is the same for the women who have been killed for drug debts inside prison, because that exists and happens. It is like a way of disciplining the rest, see? The money arrives once a month, that is, once a month those who want to consume have the possibility of expecting money.

But, how do you take out the money?
In the Ezeiza Prison, how it works is that you work and you get paid for 200 hours, it depends, sometimes you work less and sometimes you work more, but the money is withdrawn in the penitentiary. Once a week the administration authorizes the money that they give you in cash, they give you a hearing and they give you a paper that says "I authorize so and so with such and such an ID number to withdraw a certain amount of money," and then you authorize someone from outside to come and withdraw that money and that's how it works.

But in the case of someone who sells things to consume inside?
They bring the money in from the outside. I was in debt in that sense and more, I started consuming more in prison than when I was on the streets, because I fell prisoner for problems of consumption. It's not that I went out to steal to be able to eat, even if I come from the lower class, I didn't rob to eat, I would rob to pay for drugs and inside I worked to continue consuming, and it meant taking out debt every month because I would pay and would immediately buy more.

Where do you currently work?
I have four jobs, I work as a cleaner in three places, in private homes. And I give workshops in Prison Unit 47. Well, now those are over, but I was working in that. Yesterday we started, we inaugurated you could say, a cooking enterprise through the YoNoFui collective. With a few other compañeras we made food to sell in an event in a social center and that is the start of a cooking project with formerly incarcerated women who are now free. That's what I prefer. I've been offered other jobs where I would have to complete an eight-hour workday and that seemed impos-

sible for me, so I didn't accept them, in these jobs I have a certain amount of flexibility.

Are you in debt now?

Now along with debts on my utility bills, I have debt from my phone. I bought a telephone, that I had to buy with a card in Coppel, because I don't have a credit card and I couldn't pay it all up front, so I bought it like that. I made three payments. So, the telephone was 3000 pesos, but buying it with that card and paying in installments it was 6800, more than twice what the telephone would be worth up front! But I made three payments and couldn't keep paying and I got a phone call from a lawyer and I just told her "I'm not working, I'm not going to pay you because I don't have a job," and also I have debts with the electricity and water companies. It was a pretty complicated situation because I didn't know that I had that debt. I live with my two sisters, and we pay the bills together, but the one in charge of paying the electricity bills hasn't been doing it for months. I got home one day and they had cut off the electricity, I called the electrical company and they told me we hadn't paid the bill in months.

What impediments do you face in your life due to debt today?

What frustrates me now is not having time, that I don't even have enough time to pay for my studies. Since I am a single mother, I can't pay a babysitter to be able to go study, nor can I pay for the readings, and I can't put my head in it because I am under so much pressure. This year I started two classes at the University of Buenos Aires, I started to do the readings and everything, but with my head about to explode, I couldn't make it work.

How does debt function from your point of view?

It makes it so that we are the ones who have to sacrifice our bodies and spend money and we don't have the option of choosing, or complaining if the things we buy are expensive or not. We have to pay anyway. I paid 37 pesos for milk today but I had to buy it anyways. We are subjected to having to pay without any exceptions, beyond any complaints I could make of the prices, I am tied to that inflation, those austerity measures, and I go into debt no matter what the costs. So we women are those who are involuntarily subjected to paying usurious interest rates and thus we are financing more power and more time for the patriarchy!

"It is worth looking for the money from anywhere in order to pay on time"

The city of La Plata is surrounded by one of the country's largest belts of fruit and vegetable production. That is where small producers are organizing in the Unión de Trabajadorxs de la Tierra (Land Workers' Union, UTT). The UTT is a national organization made up of thousands of small producers and peasants that, through local groups or nodes, produces organic food, intervenes in distribution networks, and organizes farmers' markets. It has been characterized by its public interventions called "verdurazos," taking in public spaces and freely distributing vegetables. The UTT has also organized to demand access to land for small producers and against the productive model of agribusiness, based on the extensive use of agrotoxins. We talk to a group of women about their intensive farm labor, constantly juggling activities and accounts to be able to live off what they produce, and disputing decisions about production, as well as how debt is a fundamental apparatus for chaining the earth to agrotoxins and transgenic seeds.

There are two: FIE and Cordial Negocios. Cordial Negocias has interest rates through the roof, but FIE is a little more accessible. And Cordial is through Banco Ciudad ...

What did you use the loan for? What type of work do you do?
Now I take care of my daughter, I'm a housewife. But it was my child's father who took out the loan, since it was for the farm. I think it was for seedlings and things like that, money is always being invested in the farm. But it's not easy! Listen, they look at how much risk there is, what you are going to plant, they ask for a guarantee, that you own property or rent or have something of value.

They'll give you a loan with just a rental contract?
I think so, because he got it with the rent contract. My dad acted as a guarantor since he had already taken out loans there, but my dad doesn't own any property or anything.

Is the finance agency here close to the farms?
Yes, it's close by, in Olmos, at the corner of 44 and 198.

Are the interests very high?
It depends because you have some with monthly payments and some with quarterly payments. He had taken out the one with payments every four months and sometimes it would get complicated, because tomatoes, for example, don't come out like that (snaps her fingers), but they take a while, they have their process.

Then his sister loaned him money. No matter what, when you go past the due date, for example, we paid on the 15th of every month, they raise the interest a lot. Well, we thought that it was a lot, but it's not even 10 pesos a day.

That's the penalty for non-payment, in comparison with a bank, the interest is really high. Later we can look into that more.

Yeah, I'm sure. We haven't taken out a loan from a bank because it is more complicated.

Have any of you had to get another extra job to pay one off one of those loans?
Yeah. Well, that is the case of my family member (laughter), who is a nurse. And I don't know if they ended up paying, but they got in deep. Really deep, I would say, because they even facilitate lending you money like that. But lately with the increase in the dollar, interest rates are high, and that's why I think it started adding up for her year by year.

And have you taken out any loans?
Yes, I have, but not much. I took one out to invest in the farm, because there was a storm and hail had fallen. The hail ruined the tarps, as well as the vegetables outside. It destroyed everything, there was nothing left.

Of course, because let's imagine that I hadn't taken out any loans up until now, that I am all paid up. But what happens tomorrow if there is a hail storm that ruins my outside crops, those that I am about to harvest, and everything I invested in the seeds that I fertilized, everything that I did to prepare the earth. All of that has a high cost. It is not easy to maintain, today it is not easy to maintain a farm, especially if you don't have your own tractor.

Let's calculate it. The tray of lettuce has almost 300 little squares. A seedling costs 150 pesos.

And lettuce is the cheapest, imagine bell peppers, tomatoes, the tray is 1500 or 2500.

So you took out a loan because of the hail?
Yes, I needed money because I was broke, and I had to pay, I had to till the vegetables again. Everything was destroyed, all shredded up.

And the interest rate was very high then?
Yeah, because this time we borrowed 25 thousand and we returned something like 52 thousand.

And did you end up defaulting, what happened?
Well, you have to work more! In odd jobs or anything that pays.

Yeah, you even go, you make a budget, let's say that you have already made two or three payments and you say "I want to pay up to this date and how much do I have to pay out of the 25,000 that I took out." If you pay it back faster, the interest is less, much less, but where are you going to get all that money from? You're not going to go out and start stealing.

So, at that time, you had to take on more odd jobs.
Yes, sometimes working at night without sleeping.

Yeah, I even work in cleaning, I care for an old woman. Because at this time I can't live off the farm alone. I don't have much land. My husband, my children, and I work on the farm. We don't hire more people because you have to pay them and give them food and my pockets aren't that deep. So I prefer to sacrifice my family and that we sustain ourselves however we can.

Have you also taken out loans?
Yes, a long time ago. But it was also for the farm. It was to start planting tomatoes. Tomatoes are the most costly, the most expensive, and they take time as well.

Yes, and the agrochemicals are very expensive.

You don't feel it so much when you go to pay for it, but when you add up all the costs, it ends up being more than half, and if you miss a payment by just one day, they charge you a separate interest.

Have you had any problems of not being able to pay?
Yes, but I made family members loan me money because you absolutely have to pay on that date or else they charge you more interest. In other words, it is worth looking for the money from anywhere in order to pay on time.

You also get a document letter with threats. Like that neighbor who had taken out like 30,000 pesos in loans and she paid back half and her ex-husband, the father of her children, had to pay the other half and he didn't do it. But she didn't have any way of proving that. She had moved on with her life, she had another partner, and they worked in something else, she didn't work on the farm anymore. But they kept on pursuing her and the guarantor, her sister. And she had no way of proving that the one who owed the money was her ex-husband.

And who are the people going after her?
The same people who go to your farm to interview you. They also say things like "we are going to take away your belongings," personal belongings, even if you don't have big things.

She was working on the farm when they took out the loan, but she separated from her ex because he was abusive, because of gender-based violence.

So, she separated because of gender-based violence, but she was left with her husband's debt?
Yep. And she doesn't want to see her ex anymore, because he has a lawyer.

Another thing that happens, is that they ask for proof of your card for the Universal Child Allowance or the Complementary Social Wage and they say that they are going to confiscate that money, which is impossible. We accompanied that compañera to the office of the Secretary of Gender with our lawyer, and the lawyer advised her: "they can't take your money from Anses, that company can't take away your Complementary Social Wage."

But, they told her that they were going to break into her house and take everything, clean her out. I don't know if the things she had there would even be enough to cover the 30,000 that she supposedly owed, it was a way of scaring her.

That's the thing, they scare you, they intimidate you. I worked there with the children, imagine, they're just kids. And, to make matters worse, she had been robbed twice. Someone broke into her house at night and broke everything. They are little wood houses, see?

They requested my husband's title on the car as a guarantee. They do that when you take out your first loan, if you have never received a loan from anywhere before. If you have already taken one out and paid off that debt, then you have more chances because if you are considered reliable, if you don't fall behind on your payments or if you pay in advance, then they offer you a little more. Suppose that I took out 20 or 30, they would increase your credit to 50, they say. We started renting with that. If not, it would be impossible to rent.

When you are at the penultimate payment, they go ahead and offer to give you another loan. Thus when they see you as more reliable, they offer you more.

Now Banco Ciudad has changed, because they give you a card and you go make a deposit at the bank, you no longer personally go to the place where the money goes. You can't pay in advance or anything because they just have a date and you pay.

There is another company, I forget its name, that we wanted to get a loan from because the interest rates were low, but they make you go through a lot of hoops. They ask for your electricity bill, they ask for the bill of sale for the seeds that you are going to buy, for the pesticides. They ask for everything.

Do you all take out loans to pay for agrotoxins as well?
Of course, if not, they are impossible to access.

And how much do the agrotoxins cost? For example, how much is a bottle of fertilizer?

Now it is more than 1000 for a small bottle. Or, between 1000 and 5000 pesos.

And it is to reproduce what is already there. That is why other compañeras are considering organic farming.

Yes, because the conventional system requires thousands and thousands of pesos, because the prices are in dollars, therefore you need a lot of money.

Conventional refers to farming with agrotoxins?
There are fewer costs if you produce organically, you could say that it gives you a certain freedom. And the results are much better, it is different. And you save a lot of money. For example, if you want to plant spinach, you invest, say, 100 pesos and with the organic system, you buy the seedlings, or the seeds, rather, and nothing else. To fertilize it, you do it yourself with your own supplies or materials that you already have. In other words, you use resources that you already have.

As women, we have been looking at how this model really affects health.

I have a problem from the sun and the agrotoxins and I cannot see a doctor because the health insurance doesn't work and also I'm not paying.

My father was poisoned curing tomatoes, because he didn't wear a face mask, the boss didn't give him one, he thought it was too expensive. My uncle and brother managed to drink milk. I don't know what it is, but milk does something and you drink it and it can make you better. But my dad didn't drink any and later he started to feel bad and his head hurt and he started to feel like he was going to throw up and foam starting coming out of his mouth and he had to go to the hospital. He was poisoned.

I stopped working with poisons a long time ago, for economic reasons, I didn't have money for that. We have started to work with the organic model, and it is going better. I keep paying off the debt that I had, I had taken out loans from FIE and Cordial.

What had you taken them out for?

To build a greenhouse, which was blown away by the wind. So I abandoned the farm, just two months ago. I was working but my husband had an accident and I couldn't pay anymore. Curing the products made me feel bad, it made me dizzy. Sometimes my son would help me but since he's still little, I can't really ask him to. In the mornings I would often do the curing by myself and I would get nausea, vomiting, headaches, and later I would take an Ibuprofen and I would feel better.

And you are still paying off that debt?
Yeah, I am still paying it. It is twice as much as what I took out.

Did you also have to look for more work to pay off that debt?
Yes, my husband worked more odd jobs and used that to pay off the loan. But he had an accident doing one of those jobs, he fell.

Yeah, we also go into debt to pay for seeds.

We don't have an education, we can't work in anything else besides the farm. And on the farm, sometimes vegetables are worth it and sometimes not, because sometimes you have to throw them out and you can't sell them, you have to keep planting no matter what. And if you don't have money, you have no other choice but to take out a loan.

Did you also go into debt?
Yes. Once I took out a loan when a storm destroyed everything, in order to get things going again, and later another storm came and knocked everything down again. So then I took out another loan to be able to keep going because, if not, what am I going to do? What will I live off of? I have three kids, I have to maintain them. My children are studying.

Today you have to graduate from primary school to be able to sweep, for example to sweep the streets.

Who generally resorts to agrochemicals? Men, it is mostly men. There are people who are very quiet, who don't say anything, and the señor who you work for says "do this" and they do it and call him the boss, but it's not like that. Everyone thinks that you work for him, that he is your boss, but he is really your business partner. Because he puts up half the money, and we are the ones who break our backs working, and nobody recognizes any of that. Everyone discriminates against you, calling you racist names and all that.

The percentage you get depends on the form of work. The sharecropper gets 50% and the other 50%, after rent, goes to the person who bankrolls you. And then you have day labor, that currently pays 800 pesos a day without food.

Not to mention that the state took away the public policies that regularized small producers, such as the Monotributo Social Agropecuario [which incorporated these small farmers into the state's pension plans]. Macri's government eliminated that program, which at least enabled us to be formal workers.

There is something else. When you have debt, even if you are being mistreated, you cannot separate from your partner. That happened to me, you see? Threats were made against my children, or that they are going to take away all of my things, that is why I couldn't get a divorce.

Debt forces you to stay.
Of course. Since you are indebted, you can't leave, and I have to continue like that and think about the future.

And you all didn't take out loans through the UTT?
They are indebted up to their underwear (laughter).

I took out a loan to buy seeds and I bought lettuce, I took out 20,000 pesos and bought everything.

What do they require in order to be able to take out a loan?
They asked for two witnesses and the authorization of my delegate.

Two witnesses or two guarantors?

Two guarantors (laughter).

What does the UTT credit consist of?
We created a system so that the organization's base takes responsibility for the situation, so that if a compañero or compañera needs something

and they have a problem, the local group, the assembly group in which they participate, discusses it, debates and figures out how to resolve it. You return the amount so that it can be loaned to someone else. It is only used for that and so if someone doesn't return it, it's one less possibility for someone else. So you take it out, but the base takes responsibility. If something happens to the compañero or compañera playing bingo, or doing something, among everyone they will be able to collectively fix it, everything is put up for discussion, it is talked about. We had to do this because last time, there were still a ton of people who didn't pay.

That's why in our base group, we don't do it, the delegate directly said no: "I am not going to be responsible for that." Actually, we had already tried it, we ended up having to pay out of our own pockets, why would I pay out of my own pocket if all I have is my own debt? My children are studying, and I also want more education, I want to study, why would I pay for someone else? It's not fair, it is not fair, therefore we are in agreement about that. If a compañero wants to take out a loan, they have to put down a title, just like we did when we started.

There's no title because it is from the organization. It is a fund that belongs to everyone. There is no "Mr. UTT" who says "yes, I present my title." It is not your money. Then, what can we do? How can we use this responsibly? Well, that is the challenge. Everyone thinks about it a lot, but it comes with responsibility, the responsibility of saying "I need money for production, I know that I am going to be able to repay it." It has very little interest, in other words, the money belongs to everyone. How can we do it?

Is it still very little in relation to people's needs?
It's nothing, it's not a massive tool. They give you a little like that and between your problems with so-and-so and, or someone's death, that's it. That compañero didn't pay you back, because they had an accident or whatever and now the money can't be returned.

"Young people's labor trajectories are very discontinuous, but their debts remain pending"

We talk to Clarisa Gambera, the current Secretary of Gender of the CTA-A (Central de Trabajadres de Argentina-Autónoma) in Buenos Aires and a member of the commission on childhood and territory. Argentina's Workers' Central Union was founded in 1992, in the midst of rising unemployment and the informalization of work in the country. It is made up of both unions and social organizations and groups of retirees. It declares itself as politically autonomous from governments, bosses, and political parties. Here Clarisa discusses how the quick and expensive "offers" of credit for youth who have only recently started precarious jobs end up making their incomes even more precarious. **Work and income are intermittent, but not debt.** *People go into debt for multiple reasons: to obtain the guarantee to be able to rent, to face the arrival of a child, to buy domestic appliances, cell phones, clothes, or a motorcycle to have some sort of labor "autonomy."*

From your labor union experience in the sphere of "childhood and territory," can you tell us how debt affects teenagers and young people today?

Now my job is to accompany young people, 18-year-olds coming out of institutions. After having been housed in shelters or other institutions, due to their age, they must initiate an autonomous exit, they have to seek employment, which is more complicated in times of high unemployment. Many of them can't do it, in many cases they haven't finished high school. If they manage to find formal employment, it is usually with low wages and highly variable hours. These are jobs with low levels of specialization, high rotation of tasks, and only in certain areas. What happens is that, a few months after receiving their first paycheck, the offer for credit appears. A bank makes the offer by mail and they also tend to go to the cleaning companies where many of these youth work. They are characterized, as we know, by high interest rates and by offering payment plans, usually in 36 installments, which makes them accessible.

What type of consumption is debt used for? In what time frames do people go into debt?

It allows them to access goods that are expensive in relation to their wages: sports clothes, sneakers, electronic goods, and household appliances. The quota that is taken out of their paycheck does not exceed 30% of a low wage. The state offers different forms of assistance to youth that make up what is needed for rent and what is left of one's wage goes to cover food and transportation. State assistance has time limits and debt always lasts longer than the subsidy. Frequently, the labor trajectories of young men and women are very intermittent, so they go through long periods of not having work, but they stay in debt. Later they work informally, but if they manage to go back to formal work with an official pay slip, they will automatically have part of their wages garnished because they are in debt. Many times the kids know this but they forget, they don't take it into account, until money is effectively docked from their paycheck, and their wages that are already quite low, become even lower because of the money that is taken out to pay back debts. Thus, since their labor trajectories are very discontinuous, debts remain pending and many times, finding themselves without an income, they have to sell back (for less money than they paid for) the things they had bought, but they still keep paying for them. This situation of automatically garnishing wages makes them question if it is worth maintaining jobs that tend to be precarious, without much expectation of promotion or training.

Could we say that the nexus between state assistance, precarious labor, and youth is being exploited by financial mechanisms? What types of violent situations does type of debt lead to? Are there differences between the guys and the girls?
The credit cards are part of a larger bankarization project, which, in the case of the guys, usually starts from the moment of one's first job. In the case of young women, it starts when they become mothers and can access the Universal Child Allowance. They often can't find jobs because it is very difficult to find opportunities to make employment compatible with childcare and even more so for groups who have little or no support network because they grew up in institutions far from their families for different reasons. In these cases, they are offered credit that they tend to use to buy cell phones and household appliances, as well as clothing for their children. Among the young people we work with, being able to buy household appliances and furniture to establish a household is a common motive for going into debt. These installments can be paid with the "subsidy for autonomous exit" that up until now lasts for a maximum of one year; this allows those who have jobs to not have to use their wages to make their debt payments. But this orderly system is often overcome by the desire for consumption of the young men and women who have lived through deprivation, so buying sneakers, sports clothing, cell phones, electronic equipment, is also a less-planned reason for going into debt and then wages are also used to pay it off.

Along with promoters, is credit offered by cell phones, by financial agencies in the neighborhoods?
There are other forms of debt through Italcred or Credial credit cards, which have very few requirements and high interest rates, that tend to be used to finance major expenses. A motorcycle is one of those expenses. Motorcycles are bought from franchises in installments plans with the goal of working in delivery and part of your wages go toward making those installment payments. For young men, the motorcycle represents the possibility of having "autonomy" in the job search. It allows them to move about, they supply their own vehicle and they generally work informally. When the motorcycle breaks or is robbed, or if they are injured, they don't get paid, and if they don't get paid they don't have any way of making their payments.

Young people also tend to go into debt to get the supplies needed for a baby: a stroller, crib, etc. These are young mothers and fathers who have to get ready for a child's arrival, they only have low wages, generally the father's, and they go into debt since they tend to buy everything necessary, because the guys feel that, by doing so, they are taking responsibility. In general, the aspects of how everyday life is sustained in cases of the most impoverished couples involve the Universal Child Allowance, the housing subsidy, for which they have priority, and also the social card. The state has a series of subsidies and programs for mothers, with the emphasis on protecting children. Another debt that appears in the case of young people who have obtained a formal job is the installment payments for the rent guarantee. If they dream of renting something, and taking into account that they come from families that don't own property, the only option is to go into debt to obtain a bank guarantee that is garnished from their wages month by month.

In your role as a union delegate, do you see the situation of indebtedness as an increasingly common condition among waged workers? How so? What are the implications?
In the union, we have not conducted a systematic study of the impact of this phenomenon of debt on the wages of our compañeras and compañeros. When we started to inquire, I found that in my work team, made up mostly of young professional women with precarious wages and jobs, with more than one job in all our cases, all of us are in debt: from credit cards or pre-approved credit from the bank where our wages

go. We go into debt to pay for vacations, to buy a new car – in all these cases to exchange affordable cars for newer models – to finance home improvements, and to be able to buy domestic appliances. Cell phones are also a necessary tool for our type of work and in every case we buy them in installments. Those who are studying go into debt to pay for books. Last winter, something new appeared: financing one's use of gas. I am in debt. I bought Christmas presents in installments, I paid for my vacation travel in installments, and I exchanged my car with a title loan that is for 18 months.

"Poor families started to be very afraid that their names would be legally implicated as debtors"

The feminist strike in Manaos on March 8, 2018, in the heart of the Brazilian Amazon, took a unique shape: they decided to occupy the building of Electrobras, the power station, to protest against its privatization and its non-acceptance of the social rate. Manaos's landscape is also unique: an emporium of natural resources dotted with Chinese assembly plants and the epicenter of trafficking in young girls. We speak to Antonia Barroso, of the Foro Permanente de Mujeres de Pernambuco, a feminist space for women in the Brazilian state of Pernambuco, organized as a platform that brings together different collectives, with nodes of the network articulated across different cities. She explains why the women's strike was organized against rate increases that generate mandatory debt, demonstrating how the banks intervene in the legal processes tied to those debts, to exploit those increases twice over. The financialization of basic services is also carried out through mass indebtedness and the moral threat of creating a legal record of those debts.

Tell us what the 8M was like in Manaos.
On March 8, we, the women of the Amazons, of the Foro Permanente de Mujeres de Manaos Brasil, occupied the building of the subsidiary of Electrobras, Brazil's state energy company. We are opposed to its privatization because we understand that privatization has an impact on our public goods and an even greater impact on women's everyday lives. Furthermore, it has an impact on the lives of working women who are heads of households who earn a salary, who get paid minimum wage, or who sometimes don't even have that wage and depend on their husbands or other family members. Therefore, I think that those families have the

right to pay a social rate, and that was another reason why we occupied the power plant and went on strike.

In addition to the threat of privatizing the energy company, what was the deal with the improper charges above what they owed that people received on their bills?
People thought that the social rate was increasing, but it was confirmed that the company was issuing an undue charge for months. They issued that improper charge through a *cartorio*. The company contracted a *cartorio* to make that charge.

What is a *cartorio*?
Cartorio is a space for civil documentation of complaints. Using this mechanism, the company started to charge families through a system of overseers, and poor families started to be very afraid that their names would be legally implicated as debtors.

Who went to collect that charge?
It was Banco ITAU, they sent the letters, the threats.

So if you wanted to pay, you had to go to Banco ITAU?
Exactly, but at first the bank didn't show up on the bill. So, families would receive a document saying they had to pay up in order to get out of that debt. What did they do? They paid that debt in the *cartorio*, they would negotiate that debt in the *cartorio* so that they would not receive a formal complaint, this caused a snowball effect because they would prefer to spend money, which they often don't have, to pay a *cartorio* so that their name isn't stained.

And how did they pay if they didn't have the money?
They would ask a family member to loan them money or they would use savings that they had planned to use on their homes. Money, for example, for buying food, is used as a resource to pay off the debt. They did all of this because they were afraid that the family's name would be involved in legal proceedings.

So, you were protesting against two things: against privatization and against those improper charges?

Yes, we created a document that we delivered to the energy company and the public ministry. We made a list of complaints about those improper charges. Additionally, after the coup led by Michel Temer, the company ended up being sold. What we know is that it is a Chinese company and that they were already negotiating with subsidiary companies and that the contract was already being closed. What the government ended up offering these companies as compensation was that for eight years they would not conduct investigations about the company's value. They also committed themselves to not continuing the program "Luz para todxs" that gave electricity access to the most remote communities in the Amazon. So, many families who live off of fishing, have no way of storing the products that they are going to sell and they have been forced to migrate.

It not only means the loss of production, but also having to move to the city.
Yes, it depends on production and also the impact on young people's lives because of the issue of school. Families would have to migrate to other cities and that is already happening.

And why did you decide to occupy the energy company last March 8?
Because March 8 represents a day of struggle and state and institutional violence are also part of this process of struggle. Due to the violence that women suffer due to the state's absence, due to the lack of accompaniment and safety, we went on strike for women's right to a life with dignity. When we speak of women, we are also talking about women who have families, whether they have male partners or not, whether or not they have children. We suffer this impact on a daily basis. Therefore, it was a day marked by all those struggles and there is nothing better than people occupying that space.

Did it end up being privatized?
As far as we know that process has concluded, there are 14 subsidiaries that are in the process of privatization. Those fourteen are from the northern and northeastern region of Brazil.

All by Chinese companies?
Yes, as far as we know, with that same company.

And what happened with the legal cases that were being established, with the threats that were arriving via the *cartorio* and the bank? Did people end up paying those or not?
When we occupied Electobras we had a meeting with the president of the subsidiary, and he promised that those families who were denouncing that improper charge were going to be reviewed case by case, but up until now they have not been called. Therefore we concluded that they had no interest in negotiating with those families.

So the role of the bank was only to make threats, as well as the bank collects the bills?
Yes, you have to pay all your bills in the bank, but additionally, that bill with a surcharge was specifically carried out by a bank through the *cartorio*. The *cartorio* would emit a document and the families had to negotiate and pay in a bank with interests. On March 8 we were able to denounce that.

Manifestos

June 2, 2017

On May 10, as we were constituting a collective body in the Plaza de Mayo to demonstrate our counter-power in opposition to impunity for crimes of state terrorism, the Alianza Cambiemos government compromised the lives of future generations by taking out billions of dollars in debt. This is the same permission that was taken by the last civil-military dictatorship by force of blood, torture, kidnapping, disappearances, extermination, and the appropriation of children. Those who carried out genocide and their accomplices silenced dissident voices and, usurping the government, took out debt, confiscated the power of labor and production, and made this power serve capital. And when we denounce impunity for the perpetrators of the genocide, which has been upheld by this government, they put us back in debt.

This simultaneity of events compels us to shout: debt is another form of violence that puts our lives at risk. Since the Alianza Cambiemos government took power, we have entered a new cycle of indebtedness, with the government borrowing nearly ninety-five billion dollars. This enormous debt is estimated to reach sixty percent of GDP by the end of 2017.

As women, we know, we have learned in our everyday lives, what it means to be in debt. We know that with debt we can't say no when we want to say no. And that the state's debt always spills over to subjugate us. And our children. And our grandchildren. It exposes us to higher levels of precarity and to new forms of violence. To take out this debt, the state promises programs to make labor flexible and reduce public spending that disproportionately affect women.

But additionally, we are users, whether voluntarily or not, of the financial system: in recent years, we were forced into the banking system, to the point that benefits from the state have become inputs for the financial system. As female heads of household, we occupy a central role in the organization and self-management of networks of cooperation.

Financial corporations exploit these community economies by charging commissions on benefits and wages and applying exorbitant interest rates on loans, credit cards, and microcredit.

However, it is with a credit card that we celebrate a birthday, with a loan that we build an addition to our house, with a microcredit loan that we seek to start the business that would enable us to survive. And thus we spend our nights poring over accounts, separating out the lion's share. That day-to-day accounting is what becomes abstract in financial policies, but as women we put our bodies on the line when we are struggling to make ends meet. How will we be able to stop male violence when we are subjected to paying debts under the threat of losing everything, and when any imbalance in the fragile economic structure in which we live leaves us out in the open and exposed? If we go to a shelter so that we can survive this violence, how will we pay the bills the following day?

Finance, through debt, constitutes a form of direct exploitation of women's labor power, vital potency, and capacity for organization in the household, the neighborhood, and the territory. The feminization of poverty and the lack of economic autonomy caused by debt make male violence even stronger.

The women's movement has consolidated itself as a dynamic and transversal social actor capable of bringing diverse forms of economic exploitation to the forefront. We stop being merely victims precisely because we are able to make the ways in which they exploit us, as well as our collective action against multiple forms of dispossession, comprehensible. In the two women's strikes that we organized in less than a year, together with women trade unionists and all types of organizations, we were able to put on the agenda and assemble the demands of formal workers and the unemployed, the demands of popular economies along with the historical demand for the recognition of the unremunerated tasks that women perform. We called for politicizing care work and recognizing self-managed work. In this context, we believe it is necessary to go further in taking stock of the renewed forms of exploitation that pauperize our living conditions and make our existence precarious, because in this context, the number of femicides has doubled. There is an intimate relation between these numbers.

As producers of value, we say: Not One Woman Less, We Want To Stay Alive and Debt Free!

WE WANT TO BE DEBT FREE! BY EVA REINOSO
— YONOFUI COLLECTIVE

December 2017
Indebted by our everyday economy, austerity encloses us more and more in a vicious circle where we cannot say NO. We cannot say no to working longer hours for less pay, to buying less for much more.

We are all conditioned. On the one hand, the single mothers, who will surely suffer exploitation and precarious labor, and women workers in the household, "housewives" who will be left totally exposed and subjected to machismo because they have to economically depend on their husbands and because they don't have the resources to achieve their autonomy. This is one of the worst forms of violence: to not be able to say no to submission because you are obligated to guarantee a plate of food for your kids.

One supposes that the state should guarantee more resources, to make sure that our rights are respected. But the only thing that the state guarantees with this debt is more oppression and violence in all the spheres that pass through daily: we pay 9 pesos for a bus ticket, 32 for a kilo of bread, 25 for a liter of milk. The Health and Public Assistance Centers don't have any supplies and are increasingly less professional, meaning service is worse each time. Electricity, water, gas, the rent: impossible to pay! You have to choose what debt is left for next month, because you know you cannot pay all the bills this month.

This debt condemns us to remaining trapped in the circuit of consumption managed by capital, in which the profit margins are excessively unnecessary, sustaining the rise of its capital, as we become the ones who involuntarily finance more power in the times of the patriarchy.

Bibliography

Berniell, Inés, Dolores de la Mata, and Matilde Pinto Machado. 2017 "The Impact of a Permanent Income Shock on the Situation of Women in the Household: The Case of a Pension Reform in Argentina." CEDLAS Working Paper No. 2018. La Plata, Argentina: CEDLAS.

Biscay, Pedro. 2015. "Dictadura, democracia y finanzas," speech given at the Central Bank of the Argentine Republic on March 25, 2015.

Blanco, Camila, Biscay, Pedro, and Freire, Alejandra. 2018. *Taller N°1 de Endeudamiento Popular: Notas para la difusión de derechos de usuarios y usuarias financieros*. Buenos Aires: Ediciones del Jinete Insomne.

Brown, Wendy. 2015. *Undoing the Demos: Neoliberalism's Stealth Revolution.* New York: Zone Books.

Caffentzis, George. 2013. "Reflections on the History of Debt Resistance: The Case of El Barzón," *South Atlantic Quarterly* 112 (4): 824–30.

—— 2018. *Los límites del capital. Deuda, moneda y lucha de clase.* Buenos Aires: Tinta Limón and Rosa Luxemburg Foundation.

Cavallero, Lucía and Gago, Verónica. 2018. "*Sacar del clóset a la deuda: 'por qué el feminismo hoy confronta a las finanzas?',*" prologue to George Caffentzis, *Los límites del capital. Deuda, moneda y lucha de clases.* Buenos Aires: Tinta Limón and Rosa Luxemburg Foundation.

Cooper, Melinda. 2017. *Family Values. Between Neoliberalism and the New Social Conservatism.* New York: Zone Books.

Durand, Cédric. 2018. *El capital ficticio.* Barcelona: NED and Futuro Anterior.

Federici, Silvia. 2012. "From Commoning to Debt: Microcredit, Student Debt and the Disinvestment in Reproduction," talk given at Goldsmith University, November 12.

—— 2016. "From Commoning to Debt: Financialization, Micro-Credit and the Changing Architecture of Capital Accumulation," www.cadtm.org/From-Commoning-to-Debt (accessed August 28, 2020).

Foucault, Michel. 2018 [1973]. *The Punitive Society: Lectures at the Collège de France, 1972–1973.* Edited by Bernard E. Harcourt and Graham Burchell. New York: Picador.

Gago, Verónica. 2015. "Financialization of Popular Life and the Extractive Operations of Capital: A Perspective from Argentina." Translated by Liz Mason-Deese. *South Atlantic Quarterly* 114 (1): 11–28.

—— 2017. *Neoliberalism from Below: Popular Pragmatics and Baroque Economies.* Translated by Liz Mason-Deese. Durham: Duke University Press Books.

—— 2018. "Is There a War 'On' the Body of Women? Finance, Territory, and Violence." Translated by Liz Mason-Deese. *Viewpoint Magazine*, www.

viewpointmag.com/2018/03/07/war-body-women-finance-territory-violence/ (accessed August 28, 2020).

Gago, Verónica and Roig, Alexandre. 2019. "Las finanzas y las cosas," in *El imperio de las finanzas. Deuda y desigualdad*. Buenos Aires: Miño y Dávila.

Galindo, María. 2004. "Las exiliadas del neoliberalismo," La Paz: Mujeres Creando.

Giraldo, César, ed. 2017. *Economía popular desde abajo*. Bogotá: Desde Abajo.

Godreau-Aubert, Ariadna. 2018. *Las propias: apuntes para una pedagogía de las endeudadas*. Cabo Rojo: Editorial Educación Emergente.

Graeber, David. 2011. *Debt: The First 5,000 Years*. Brooklyn, NY: Melville House.

Guisoni, Oscar. 2012. "Plan para dinamitar la deuda," *Página/12*, www.pagina12.com.ar/2001/01-07/01-07-03/pag21.htm (accessed August 28, 2020).

Harvey, David. 2003. *The New Imperialism*. Oxford: Oxford University Press.

Lazzarato, Maurizio. 2012. *The Making of the Indebted Man: An Essay on the Neoliberal Condition*. Translated by Joshua David Jordan. Los Angeles: Semiotext(e).

Lazzarato, Maurizio. 2015. *Governing by Debt*. Translated by Joshua David Jordan. South Pasadena, CA: Semiotext.

——2020. *El capital odia a todo el mundo*. Buenos Aires: Eterna cadencia.

Lordon, Frédéric. 2010. *Willing Slaves of Capital: Spinoza and Marx on Desire*. London: Verso.

Luxemburg, Rosa. 1951 [1913]. *The Accumulation of Capital*. Translated by Agnes Schwarzchild. New York: Routledge.

Madsen, Nina. 2013. "Entre a dupla jornada e a discriminação contínua. Um olhar feminista sobre o discurso da 'nova classe média'," in Bartelt, Dawid Danilo (eds), *A "Nova Classe Média" no Brasil como Conceito e Projeto Político*. Río de Janeiro: Fundação Heinrich Böll.

Martin, Randy. 2002. *Financialization of Daily Life*. Philadelphia: Temple University Press.

Nápoli, Bruno, Perosino, Celeste, and Bosisio, Walter. 2014. *La dictadura del capital financiero. El capital militar corporativo y la trama bursátil*. Buenos Aires: Peña Lillo-Ediciones Continente.

Nietzsche, Friedrich. 2014 [1987]. *On the Genealogy of Morals*. Edited by Robert C. Holub. Translated by Michael A. Scarpitti. Reprint edition. London: Penguin Classics.

Ossandón, José, ed. 2012. "Destapando la caja negra: sociología de los créditos de consumo en Chile," Santiago: Instituto de Inves- tigación en Ciencias Sociales, ICSO, Universidad Diego Portales.

Rolnik, Raquel. 2018. *La guerra de los lugares. La colonización de la tierra y la vivienda en la era de las finanzas*. Barcelona: Descontrol.

Sassen, Saskia. 2014. *Expulsions: Brutality and Complexity in the Global Economy*. Cambridge, MA: Belknap Press: An Imprint of Harvard University Press.

Segato, Rita. 2013. *La escritura en el cuerpo de las mujeres asesinadas en Ciudad Juárez*. Buenos Aires: Tinta Limón.

Strike Debt Assembly. 2012. *The Debt Resistors Operations Manual.* New York: Common Notions. strikedebt.org/The-Debt-Resistors-Operations-Manual. pdf.

Taylor, Keeanga-Yamahtta. 2016. *From #BlackLivesMatter to Black Liberation.* Chicago: Haymarket Books.

Terranova, Tiziana. 2017. "Debt and Autonomy: Lazzarato and the Constituent Powers of the Social," *The New Reader* 1 (1).

Toro, Graciela. 2010. *La pobreza: un gran negocio.* La Paz: Mujeres Creando.

Villareal, Magdalena. 2004. *Antropología de la deuda: crédito, ahorro, fiado y prestado en las finanzas cotidianas.* Mexico City: Ma Porrúa Editor.

Zambrana, Rocío. 2019. "Rendir cuentas, pasarle la cuenta". *Revista 8ogrados.* Puerto Rico.

Index

Thanks to our Patreon Subscribers:

Abdul Alkalimat
Andrew Perry

Who have shown their generosity and comradeship in difficult times.